Jewish History, Jewish Religion

'[This is] a powerful book calling on Jews ... to face up to some abhorrent aspects of their own religious heroes and traditions ... . Israel Shahak's stirring challenge has deep relevance for Israel's present policies.' Tom Harpur, *The Toronto Star*

'This is a remarkable book. Its brevity only adds to its powerful impact. It deserves a wide readership, not only among Jews, but among Christians who seek a fuller understanding both of historical Judaism and of modern-day Israel.' Ted Schmidt, *Catholic New Times*

'Israel Shahak won fame in Israel by his principled persistence in telling truths which most Israelis don't like to hear.
  [This] book offers three central theories ... [one] is that the heritage of Jewish fanaticism, especially in the domain of Jewish attitudes toward Gentiles, is a stumbling block preventing the development of a secular and enlightened Jewish civilization.' Benyamin Beit-Hallahmi, *Haaretz*

'The real test facing both Israeli and diaspora Jews is the test of their self-criticism, which must include the critique of the Jewish past. Most disturbing, Shahak insists that the religion, in its classical and Talmudic form, is "poisoning the minds and hearts". This controversial attack of Israel by a Jew is bound to alarm Jewry worldwide.' *American Library Association Booklist*

'Let me recommend [Shahak's] latest book ... In it Shahak subjects the whole history of Orthodoxy ... to a hilarious and scrupulous critique.' Christopher Hitchens, *The Nation*

'[Shahak is] a fine scholar and Israel's foremost defender of human rights ... [this is] a ruthlessly penetrating examination of Jewish religion and history.' Ian Gilmour, *London Review of Books*

'Shahak's overview of Jewish history is both erudite and readable ... The shell containing the polemic core of the essay, in which the Jewish religion's attitude to non-Jews is exposed and dissected ... is a trail-blazing, double taboo-breaking piece of dynamite.' *Middle East International*

'Anyone who wants to change the Jewish community so that it stops siding with the forces of reaction should read this book.' Raphael Salkie, *Jewish Socialist*

'We should all be grateful that Dr Shahak has persevered and given us this important work. His message gets to the heart of U.S.–Israeli relations. It is not only Jews who should read *Jewish History, Jewish Religion*, but Christians as well.' Grace Halsell, *Middle East Policy*

'Shahak's book is among the few that are most essential to those of us interested in the Middle East.' Henry Fischer, *The Link*

Jewish History, Jewish Religion

The Weight of Three Thousand Years

Israel Shahak

Foreword by Gore Vidal

Foreword to the second printing
by Edward Said

Pluto Press

LONDON • CHICAGO, ILLINOIS

First published 1994 by Pluto Press
345 Archway Road, London N6 5AA and
1436 West Randolph, Chicago, Illinois 60607, USA

Reprinted with a new Foreword, 1997

Chapters 2, 3, 4 and 5 first appeared in the journal *Khamsin* and
are reproduced with permission
Forewords copyright © 1994 Gore Vidal and 1997 Edward Said
Copyright © 1994, 1997 Israel Shahak

British Library Cataloguing in Publication Data
A catalogue record for this book is available from the
British Library

ISBN 0 7453 0818 X hardback

Library of Congress Cataloging in Publication Data
Shahak, Israel.
    Jewish history, Jewish religion : the weight of three thousand
    years / Israel Shahak
      118pp. 22cm.
    Includes bibliographical references and index.
    ISBN 0-7453-0818-X
    1. Israel – Politics and government. 2. Orthodox Judaism
    – Israel – Controversial literature. 3. Zionism –
    Controversial literature. 4. Palestinian Arabs – Israel.
    I. Title. II. Series.
    DS102.95.S52   1994
    956.94—dc20   94–1596
                                                   CIP

2005 2004 2003 2002 2001 2000 1999 1998 1997

10   9   8   7   6   5

Designed, typeset and produced for Pluto Press by
Chase Production Service, Chadlington, OX7 3LN
Printed in the EC by Redwood Books

Contents

Foreword to the first printing
by *Gore Vidal*

Sometime in the late 1950s, that world-class gossip and occasional historian, John F. Kennedy, told me how, in 1948, Harry
S. Truman had been pretty much abandoned by everyone when
he came to run for president. Then an American Zionist
brought him two million dollars in cash, in a suitcase, aboard
his whistle-stop campaign train. 'That's why our recognition of
Israel was rushed through so fast.' As neither Jack nor I was
an antisemite (unlike his father and my grandfather) we took
this to be just another funny story about Truman and the
serene corruption of American politics.

Unfortunately, the hurried recognition of Israel as a state
has resulted in forty-five years of murderous confusion, and the
destruction of what Zionist fellow travellers thought would be a
pluralistic state – home to its native population of Muslims,
Christians and Jews, as well as a future home to peaceful
European and American Jewish immigrants, even the ones who
affected to believe that the great realtor in the sky had given
them, in perpetuity, the lands of Judea and Samaria. Since
many of the immigrants were good socialists in Europe, we
assumed that they would not allow the new state to become a
theocracy, and that the native Palestinians could live with them
as equals. This was not meant to be. I shall not rehearse the
wars and alarms of that unhappy region. But I will say that the
hasty invention of Israel has poisoned the political and intellectual life of the USA, Israel's unlikely patron.

Unlikely, because no other minority in American history has
ever hijacked so much money from the American taxpayers in
order to invest in a 'homeland'. It is as if the American
taxpayer had been obliged to support the Pope in his recon-
quest of the Papal States simply because one third of our
people are Roman Catholic. Had this been attempted, there
would have been a great uproar and Congress would have said
no. But a religious minority of less than two per cent has
bought or intimidated seventy senators (the necessary two
thirds to overcome an unlikely presidential veto) while enjoying
support of the media.

In a sense, I rather admire the way that the Israel lobby
has gone about its business of seeing that billions of dollars,
year after year, go to make Israel a 'bulwark against commu-

nism'. Actually, neither the USSR nor communism was ever much of a presence in the region. What America did manage to do was to turn the once friendly Arab world against us. Meanwhile, the misinformation about what is going on in the Middle East has got even greater and the principal victim of these gaudy lies – the American taxpayer to one side – is American Jewry, as it is constantly bullied by such professional terrorists as Begin and Shamir. Worse, with a few honourable exceptions, Jewish-American intellectuals abandoned liberalism for a series of demented alliances with the Christian (antisemitic) right and with the Pentagon–industrial complex. In 1985 one of them blithely wrote that when Jews arrived on the American scene they 'found liberal opinion and liberal politicians more congenial in their attitudes, more sensitive to Jewish concerns' but now it is in the Jewish interest to ally with the Protestant fundamentalists because, after all, 'is there any point in Jews hanging on, dogmatically, hypocritically, to their opinions of yesteryear?' At this point the American left split and those of us who criticised our onetime Jewish allies for misguided opportunism, were promptly rewarded with the ritual epithet 'antisemite' or 'self-hating Jew'.

Fortunately, the voice or reason is alive and well, and in Israel, of all places. From Jerusalem, Israel Shahak never ceases to analyse not only the dismal politics of Israel today but the Talmud itself, and the effect of the entire rabbinical tradition on a small state that the right-wing rabbinate means to turn into a theocracy for Jews only. I have been reading Shahak for years. He has a satirist's eye for the confusions to be found in any religion that tries to rationalise the irrational. He has a scholar's sharp eye for textual contradictions. He is a joy to read on the great Gentile-hating Dr Maimonides.

Needless to say, Israel's authorities deplore Shahak. But there is not much to be done with a retired professor of chemistry who was born in Warsaw in 1933 and spent his childhood in the concentration camp at Belsen. In 1945, he came to Israel; served in the Israeli military; did not become a Marxist in the years when it was fashionable. He was – and still is – a humanist who detests imperialism whether in the name of the God of Abraham or of George Bush. Equally, he opposes with great wit and learning the totalitarian strain in Judaism. Like a highly learned Thomas Paine, Shahak illustrates the prospect before us, as well as the long history behind us, and thus he continues to reason, year after year. Those who heed him will certainly be wiser and – dare I say? – better. He is the latest, if not the last, of the great prophets.

Foreword to the second printing
by *Edward Said*

Professor Israel Shahak, emeritus professor of organic chemistry at the Hebrew University in Jerusalem, is one of the most remarkable individuals in the contemporary Middle East. I first met him and began a regular correspondence with him almost twenty-five years ago, in the aftermath first of the 1967 and then the 1973 war. Born in Poland, and having survived and then escaped a Nazi concentration camp, he came to Palestine immediately after World War Two. Like all young Israelis of the time, he served in the army, and for many years served in the military reserves for a short period every summer, as Israeli law requires. Possessed of a fierce, relentlessly inquisitive and probing intellect, Shahak pursued his career as an outstanding university lecturer and researcher in organic chemistry – he was often named the best teacher by his students, and given awards for his academic performance – and at the same time began to see for himself what Zionism and the practices of the state of Israel entailed in suffering and deprivation not only for the Palestinians of the West Bank and Gaza, but for the substantial non-Jewish (i.e. Palestinian minority) people who did not leave in the expulsion of 1948, remained, and them became Israeli citizens. This then led him to a systematic inquiry into the nature of the Israeli state, its history, ideological and political discourses which, he quickly discovered, were unknown to most non-Israelis, especially Diaspora Jews for whom Israel was a marvelous, democratic, and miraculous state deserving unconditional support and defense.

He then re-established and was for several years the Chairman of the Israeli League of Human Rights, a relatively small group of like-minded people whose idea it was that human rights should be equal for everyone, not just for the Jews. It was in that specific context that I first became aware of his work. The one thing that immediately distinguished Shahak's political positions from that of most other Israeli and non-Israeli Jewish doves was that he alone stated the unadorned truth, without consideration for whether that truth, if stated plainly, might not be 'good' for Israeli or the Jews. He was profoundly, and I would say aggressively and radically, un- and anti-racist in his writings and public statements; there was one standard, and one standard only, for infractions against human rights, so it did not matter if most of the time Israeli Jews were assaulting Palestinians, since he, as an intellectual, *had* to

testify against those assaults. It is no exaggeration to say that
so strictly did he adhere to this position that he very soon
became an extremely unpopular man in Israel. I recall that
about fifteen years ago he was declared dead, although of
course he was extremely alive; the *Washington Post* reported his
'death' in a story which, after Shahak actually visited the *Post*
to prove that he was not 'dead' he gleefully told his friends,
had no effect on the *Post* which has never printed a correction!
So to some people he is still 'dead', a wish-fantasy that reveals
how uncomfortable he makes 'friends of Israel' feel.

It should also be said that Shahak's mode of telling the
truth has always been rigorous and uncompromising. There is
nothing seductive about it, no attempt made to put it 'nicely',
no effort expended on making the truth palatable, or somehow
explainable. For Shahak killing is murder is killing is murder:
his manner is to repeat, to shock, to bestir the lazy or indifferent into galvanized awareness of the human pain that they
might be responsible for. At times Shahak has annoyed and
angered people, but this is part of his personality and, it must
be said, of his sense of mission. Along with the late Professor
Yehoshua Leibowitch, a man he deeply admired and often
worked with, Shahak endorsed the phrase 'Judeo-Nazi' to char-
acterize methods used by the Israelis to subordinate and re-
press the Palestinians. Yet he never said or wrote anything that
he did not find out for himself, see with his own eyes, experience directly. The difference between him and most other
Israelis was that he made the connections between Zionism,
Judaism, and repressive practices against 'non-Jews': and of
course he drew the conclusions.

A great deal of what he writes has had the function of
exposing propaganda and lies for what they are. Israel is
unique in the world for the excuses made on its behalf: journalists either do not see or write what they know to be true
for fear of blacklisting or retaliation; political, cultural and
intellectual figures, especially in Europe and the United States,
go out of their way to praise Israel and shower it with the
greatest largesse of any nation on earth, even though many of
them are aware of the injustices of the country. They say
nothing about those. The result is an ideological smoke screen
that more than any single individual Shahak has laboured to
dissipate. A Holocaust victim and survivor himself, he knows
the meaning of anti-Semitism. Yet unlike most others he does
not allow the horrors of the Holocaust to manipulate the truth
of what in the name of the Jewish people Israel has done to
the Palestinians. For him, suffering is not the exclusive possession of one group of victims; it should instead be, but rarely is,

the basis for humanizing the victims, making it incumbent on them *not* to cause suffering of the kind that they suffered. Shahak has admonished his compatriots not to forget that an appalling history of anti-Semitism endured does not entitle them to do what they wish, just because they have suffered. No wonder then he has been so unpopular, since by saying such things, Shahak has morally undermined Israel's laws and political practises towards the Palestinians.

Shahak goes even further. He is an absolute and unwavering secularist when it comes to human history. By this I do not mean to say that he is against religion, but rather that he is against religion as a way of explaining events, justifying irrational and cruel policies, aggrandizing one group of 'believers' at the expense of the others. What is also surprising is that Shahak is not, properly speaking, a man of the left. In a whole variety of ways he is very critical of Marxism, and traces his principles to European free-thinkers, liberals, and courageous public intellectuals like Voltaire and Orwell. What makes Shahak even more formidable as a supporter of Palestinian rights is that he does not succumb to the sentimental idea that because the Palestinians have suffered under Israel they must be excused for their follies. Far from it: Shahak has always been quite critical of the PLO's sloppiness, its ignorance of Israel, its inability to resolutely oppose Israel, its shabby compromises and cult of personality, its general lack of seriousness. He has also spoken out forcefully against revenge or 'honor' killings against Palestinian women, and has always been a strong supporter of feminist liberation.

During the 1980s when it became fashionable for Palestinian intellectuals and a few PLO officers to seek out 'dialogue' with the Israeli doves of Peace Now, the Labor Party, and Meretz, Shahak was routinely excluded. For one, he was extremely critical of the Israeli peace camp for its compromises, its shameful practice of pressuring the Palestinians and not the Israeli government for changes in policy, its unwillingness to free itself from the constraints of 'protecting' Israel by not saying anything critical about it to non-Jews. For another, he was never a politician: he simply did not believe in all the posturing and circumlocutions that people with political ambitions were always willing to indulge. He fought for equality, truth, real peace and dialogue with Palestinians; the official Israeli doves fought for arrangements that would make possible the kind of peace that brought Oslo, and which Shahak was one of the first to denounce. Speaking as a Palestinian, however, I was always ashamed that Palestinian activists who were anxious to dialogue in secret or in public with the Labor Party or Meretz, refused to have anything to do with Shahak. For them he was too radical, too outspoken, too marginal with regard to offical power. Secretly, I think, they also feared that he would be too critical of Palestinian policies. He certainly would have.

Aside from his example as an intellectual who never betrayed his calling or compromised with the truth as he saw it, Shahak performed an immense service over the years for his friends and supporters abroad. Acting on the correct premise that the Israeli press was paradoxically more truthful and informative about Israel than either the Arab or Western media, he has laboriously translated, annotated, and then reproduced and also dispatched thousands of articles from the Hebrew-language press. It is impossible to over-estimate this service. For me, as someone who spoke and wrote about Palestine, I could not have done what I did without Shahak's papers and of course his example as a seeker after truth, knowledge, and justice. It is as simple as that, and I therefore owe him a gigantic debt of gratitude. He did this labor at his own expense for the most part, as well as on his own time. The footnotes he added and the little introductions that he wrote for his monthly selections from the press were invaluable for their searching wit, deeply informative pithiness, and unendingly pedagogical patience. all the while of course Shahak continued his scientific research and his teaching, neither of which had anything to do with his annotations and translations.

Somehow he also found time to become the most erudite individual I have ever known. His range of knowledge of music, literature, sociology and above all history – in Europe, Asia and elsewhere – is unrivalled in my experience. But it is as a scholar of Judaism that he towers over so many others, since it is Judaism that has occupied his energies as a scholar and political activist from the beginning. A few years ago he began interspersing his translations with Reports, that soon became monthly documents of several thousand words on one topic – for example, the real rabbinical background to Rabin's assassination, or why Israel must make peace with Syria (surprisingly because Syria is the only Arab country which can actually harm Israel militarily), and so on. These were invaluable digests of the press, plus extremely shrewd, often inspired analyses of current trends and issues, usually obscured or unreported by the mainstream media.

I have always known Shahak to be a prodigious historian, brilliant intellectual and polymath scholar, and political activist: but as I suggested above I have come to realize his central 'hobby' has been a study of Judaism, of the rabbinical and

Talmudic traditions, and of the scholarship on the subject. This book is therefore a powerful contribution to these things. It is no less than a succinct history of 'classical' as well as more recent Judaism, as those apply to an understanding of modern Israel. Shahak shows that the obscure, narrowly chauvinist prescriptions against various undesirable Others are to be found in Judaism (as well of course as other monotheistic traditions) but he also then goes on to show the continuity between those and the way Israel treats Palestinians, Christians and other non-Jews. A devastating portrait of prejudice, hypocrisy and religious intolerance emerges. What is important about it is that Shahak's description gives the lie not only to the fictions about Israel's democracy that abound in the Western media, but it also implicitly indicts Arab leaders and intellectuals for their scandalously ignorant view of that state, especially when they pontificate to their people that Israel has really changed and now wants peace with Palestinians and other Arabs.

Shahak is a very brave man who should be honored for his services to humanity. But in today's world the example of indefatigable work, unrelenting moral energy, and intellectual brilliance that he has set are an embarrassment to the status quo, and to everyone for whom the work 'controversial' means 'unwelcome' and 'unsettling'. I am certain, however, that what he says in *Jewish History, Jewish Religion* will be a source of discomfort to his Arab readers as well. I am sure he would say that he is pleased.

Chapter 1

A Closed Utopia?

> I write here what I think is true, for the stories of the Greeks are numerous and in my opinion ridiculous.
>> (Hecateus of Miletus, as quoted by Herodotus)

> Amicus Plato sed magis amica veritas – Plato is a friend but truth is a greater friend.
>> (Traditional paraphrase of a passage of Aristotle's Ethics)

> In a free state every man can think what he wants and say what he thinks.
>> (Spinoza)

This book, although written in English and addressed to people living outside the State of Israel, is, in a way, a continuation of my political activities as an Israeli Jew. Those activities began in 1965–6 with a protest which caused a considerable scandal at the time: I had personally witnessed an ultra-religious Jew refuse to allow his phone to be used on the Sabbath in order to call an ambulance for a non-Jew who happened to have collapsed in his Jerusalem neighbourhood. Instead of simply publishing the incident in the press, I asked for a meeting with the members of the Rabbinical Court of Jerusalem, which is composed of rabbis nominated by the State of Israel. I asked them whether such behaviour was consistent with their interpretation of the Jewish religion. They answered that the Jew in question had behaved correctly, indeed piously, and backed their statement by referring me to a passage in an authoritative compendium of Talmudic laws, written in this century. I reported the incident to the main Hebrew daily, Ha'aretz, whose publication of the story caused a media scandal.

The results of the scandal were, for me, rather negative. Neither the Israeli, nor the diaspora, rabbinical authorities ever reversed their ruling that a Jew should not violate the Sabbath in order to save the life of a Gentile. They added much sanctimonious twaddle to the effect that if the consequence of such an act puts Jews in danger, the violation of the Sabbath is permitted, for their sake. It became apparent to me, as drawing on knowledge acquired in my youth, I began to study the Talmudic laws governing the relations between Jews and non-Jews, that neither Zionism, including its seemingly secular part, nor Israeli politics since the inception of the State of Israel, nor particularly the policies of the Jewish supporters of Israel in the diaspora, could be understood unless the deeper influence of those laws, and the worldview which they both create and express is taken into account. The actual policies Israel pursued after the Six Day War, and in particular the apartheid character of the Israeli regime in the Occupied Territories and the attitude of the majority of Jews to the issue of the rights of the Palestinians, even in the abstract, have merely strengthened this conviction.

By making this statement I am not trying to ignore the political or strategic considerations which may have also influenced the rulers of Israel. I am merely saying that actual politics is an interaction between realistic considerations (whether valid or mistaken, whether moral or immoral in my view) and ideological influences. The latter tend to be more influential the less they are discussed and 'dragged into the light'. Any form of racism, discrimination and xenophobia becomes more potent and politically influential if it is taken for granted by the society which indulges in it. This is especially so if its discussion is prohibited, either formally or by tacit agreement. When racism, discrimination and xenophobia is prevalent among Jews, and directed against non-Jews, being fuelled by religious motivations, it is like its opposite case, that of antisemitism and its religious motivations. Today, however, while the second is being discussed, the very existence of the first is generally ignored, more outside Israel than within it.

Defining the Jewish State

Without a discussion of the prevalent Jewish attitudes to non-Jews, even the concept of Israel as 'a Jewish state', as Israel formally defines itself, cannot be understood. The widespread misconception that Israel, even without considering its regime in the Occupied Territories, is a true democracy arises from the refusal to confront the significance of the term 'a Jewish state' for non-Jews. In my view, Israel as a Jewish state constitutes a danger not only to itself and its inhabitants, but to all Jews and to all other peoples and states in the Middle East and beyond. I also consider that other Middle Eastern states or entities which define themselves as 'Arab' or 'Muslim', like the Israeli self-definition as being 'Jewish', likewise constitute a danger. However, while this danger is widely discussed, the danger inherent in the Jewish character of the State of Israel is not.

The principle of Israel as 'a Jewish state' was supremely important to Israeli politicians from the inception of the state and was inculcated into the Jewish population by all conceivable ways. When, in the early 1980s, a tiny minority of Israeli Jews emerged which opposed this concept, a Constitutional Law (that is, a law overriding provisions of other laws, which cannot be revoked except by a special procedure) was passed in 1985 by an enormous majority of the Knesset. By this law no party whose programme openly opposes the principle of 'a Jewish state', or proposes to change it by democratic means, is allowed to participate in the elections to the Knesset. I myself strongly oppose this constitutional principle. The legal consequence for me is that I cannot belong, in the state of which I am a citizen, to a party having principles with which I would agree and which is allowed to participate in Knesset elections. Even this example shows that the State of Israel is not a democracy due to the application of a Jewish ideology directed against all non-Jews and those Jews who oppose this ideology. But the danger which this dominant ideology represents is not limited to domestic affairs. It also influences Israeli foreign policies. This danger will continue to grow, as long as two currently operating developments are being strengthened: the increase in the Jewish character of Israel and the increase in its power, particularly in nuclear power. Another ominous factor is that Israeli influence in the USA political establishment is also increasing. Hence accurate information about Judaism, and especially about the treatment of non-Jews by Israel, is now not only important, but politically vital as well.

Let me begin with the official Israeli definition of the term 'Jewish', illustrating the crucial difference between Israel as 'a Jewish state' and the majority of other states. By this official definition, Israel 'belongs' to persons who are defined by the Israeli authorities as 'Jewish', irrespective of where they live, and to them alone. On the other hand, Israel doesn't officially 'belong' to its non-Jewish citizens, whose status is considered even officially as inferior. This means in practice that if members of a Peruvian tribe are converted to Judaism, and thus regarded as Jewish, they are entitled at once to become Israeli citizens and benefit from the approximately 70 per cent of the West Bank land (and the 92 per cent of the area of Israel proper), officially designated only for the benefit of Jews. All non-Jews, (not only all Palestinians) are prohibited from benefiting from those lands. (The prohibition applies even to Israeli Arabs who served in the Israeli army and reached a high rank.) The case involving Peruvian converts to Judaism actually occurred a few years ago. The newly-created Jews were settled in the West Bank, near Nablus, on land from which non-Jews are officially excluded. All Israeli governments are taking enormous political risks, including the risk of war, so that such settlements, composed exclusively of persons who are defined as 'Jewish' (and not 'Israeli' as most of the media mendaciously claims) would be subject to only 'Jewish' authority.

I suspect that the Jews of the USA or of Britain would regard it as antisemitic if Christians would propose that the USA or the United Kingdom should become a 'Christian state', belonging only to citizens officially defined as 'Christians'. The consequence of such doctrine is that Jews converting to Christianity would become full citizens because of their conversion. It should be recalled that the benefits of conversions are well known to Jews from their own history. When the Christian and the Islamic states used to discriminate against all persons not belonging to the religion of the state, including the Jews, the discrimination against Jews was at once removed by their conversion. But a non-Jew discriminated against by the State of Israel will cease to be so treated the moment he or she converts to Judaism. This simply shows that the same kind of exclusivity that is regarded by a majority of the diaspora Jews as antisemitic is regarded by the majority of all Jews as Jewish. To oppose both antisemitism and Jewish chauvinism is widely regarded among Jews as a 'self-hatred', a concept which I regard as nonsensical.

The meaning of the term 'Jewish" and its cognates, including 'Judaism', thus becomes in the context of Israeli politics as important as the meaning of 'Islamic' when officially used by Iran or 'communist' when it was officially used by the USSR. However, the meaning of the term 'Jewish' as it is popularly used is not clear, either in Hebrew or when translated into other languages, and so the term had to be defined officially.

According to Israeli law a person is considered 'Jewish' if either their mother, grandmother, great-grandmother and great-great-grandmother were Jewesses by religion; or if the person was converted to Judaism in a way satisfactory to the Israeli authorities, and on condition that the person has not converted from Judaism to another religion, in which case Israel ceases to regard them as 'Jewish'. Of the three conditions, the first represents the Talmudic definition of 'who is a Jew', a definition followed by Jewish Orthodoxy. The Talmud and post-Talmudic rabbinic law also recognise the conversion of a non-Jew to Judaism (as well as the purchase of a non-Jewish slave by a Jew followed by a different kind of conversion) as a method of becoming Jewish, provided that the conversion is performed by authorised rabbis in a proper manner. This 'proper manner' entails, for females, their inspection by three rabbis while naked in a 'bath of purification', a ritual which, although notorious to all readers of the Hebrew press, is not often mentioned by the English media in spite of its undoubted interest for certain readers. I hope that this book will be the beginning of a process which will rectify this discrepancy.

But there is another urgent necessity for an official definition of who is, and who is not 'Jewish'. The State of Israel officially discriminates in favour of Jews and against non-Jews in many domains of life, of which I regard three as being most important: residency rights, the right to work and the right to equality before the law. Discrimination in residency is based on the fact that about 92 per cent of Israel's land is the property of the state and is administered by the Israel Land Authority according to regulations issued by the Jewish National Fund (JNF), an affiliate of the World Zionist Organization. In its regulations the JNF denies the right to reside, to open a business, and often also to work, to anyone who is not Jewish, only because he is not Jewish. At the same time, Jews are not prohibited from taking residence or opening businesses anywhere in Israel. If applied in another state against the Jews, such discriminatory practice would instantly and justifiably be labelled antisemitism and would no doubt spark massive public protests. When applied by Israel as a part of its 'Jewish ideology', they are usually studiously ignored or excused when rarely mentioned.

The denial of the right to work means that non-Jews are prohibited officially from working on land administered by the Israel Land Authority according to the JNF regulations. No doubt these regulations are not always, or even often, enforced but they do exist. From time to time Israel attempts enforcement campaigns by state authorities, as, for example, when the Agriculture Ministry acts against 'the pestilence of letting fruit orchards belonging to Jews and situated on National Land [i.e., land belonging to the State of Israel] be harvested by Arab labourers', even if the labourers in question are citizens of Israel. Israel also strictly prohibits Jews settled on 'National Land' to sub-rent even a part of their land to Arabs, even for a short time; and those who do so are punished, usually by heavy fines. There is no prohibition on non-Jews renting their land to Jews. This means, in my own case, that by virtue of being a Jew I have the right to lease an orchard for harvesting its produce from another Jew, but a non-Jew, whether a citizen of Israel or a resident alien, does not have this right.

Non-Jewish citizens of Israel do not have the right to equality before the law. This discrimination is expressed in many Israeli laws in which, presumably in order to avoid embarrassment, the terms 'Jewish' and 'non-Jewish' are usually not explicitly stated, as they are in the crucial Law of Return. According to that law only persons officially recognised as 'Jewish' have an automatic right of entry to Israel and of settling in it. They automatically receive an 'immigration certificate' which provides them on arrival with 'citizenship by virtue of having returned to the Jewish homeland', and with the right to many financial benefits, which vary somewhat according to the country from which they emigrated. The Jews who emigrate from the states of the former USSR receive 'an absorption grant' of more than $20,000 per family. All Jews immigrating to Israel according to this law immediately acquire the right to vote in elections and to be elected to the Knesset – even if they do not speak a word of Hebrew.

Other Israeli laws substitute the more obtuse expressions 'anyone who can immigrate in accordance with the Law of Return' and 'anyone who is not entitled to immigrate in accordance with the Law of Return'. Depending on the law in question, benefits are then granted to the first category and systematically denied to the second. The routine means for enforcing discrimination in everyday life is the ID card, which everyone is obliged to carry at all times. ID cards list the official 'nationality' of a person, which can be 'Jewish', 'Arab', 'Druze' and the like, with the significant exception of 'Israeli'. Attempts to force the Interior Minister to allow Israelis wishing to be officially described as 'Israeli', or even as 'Israeli-Jew' in their ID cards have failed. Those who have attempted to do so have received a letter from the Ministry of the Interior stating that 'it was decided not to recognise an Israeli nationality'. The letter does not specify who made this decision or when.

There are so many laws and regulations in Israel which discriminate in favour of the persons defined as those 'who can immigrate in accordance with the Law of Return' that the subject demands separate treatment. We can look here at one example, seemingly trivial in comparison with residence restrictions, but nevertheless important since it reveals the real intentions of the Israeli legislator. Israeli citizens who left the country for a time but who are defined as those who 'can immigrate in accordance with the Law of Return' are eligible on their return to generous customs benefits, to receive subsidy for their children's high school education, and to receive either a grant or a loan on easy terms for the purchase of an apartment, as well as other benefits. Citizens who cannot be so defined, in other words, the non-Jewish citizens of Israel, get none of these benefits. The obvious intention of such discriminatory measures is to decrease the number of non-Jewish citizens of Israel, in order to make Israel a more 'Jewish' state.

The Ideology of 'Redeemed' Land

Israel also propagates among its Jewish citizens an exclusivist ideology of the Redemption of Land. Its official aim of minimizing the number of non-Jews can be well perceived in this ideology, which is inculcated to Jewish schoolchildren in Israel. They are taught that it is applicable to the entire extent of either the State of Israel or, after 1967, to what is referred to as the Land of Israel. According to this ideology, the land which has been 'redeemed' is the land which has passed from non-Jewish to Jewish ownership. The ownership can be either private, or belong to either the JNF or the Jewish state. The land which belongs to non-Jews is, on the contrary, considered to be 'unredeemed'. Thus, if a Jew who committed the blackest crimes which can be imagined buys a piece of land from a virtuous non-Jew, the 'unredeemed' land becomes 'redeemed' by such a transaction. However, if a virtuous non-Jew purchases land from the worst Jew, the formerly pure and 'redeemed' land becomes 'unredeemed' again. The logical conclusion of such an ideology is the expulsion, called 'transfer', of all non-Jews from the area of land which has to be 'redeemed'. Therefore the Utopia of the 'Jewish ideology' adopted by the State of Israel is a land which is wholly 'redeemed' and none of it is owned or worked by non-Jews. The leaders of the Zionist labour movement expressed this utterly repellent idea with the greatest clarity. Walter Laquer, a devoted Zionist, tells in his *History of Zionism*[1] how one of these spiritual fathers, A.D. Gordon, who died in 1919, 'objected to violence in principle and justified self defence only in extreme circumstances. But he and his friends wanted every tree and every bush in the Jewish homeland to be planted by nobody else except Jewish pioneers.' This means that they wanted everybody else to just go away and leave the land to be 'redeemed' by Jews. Gordon's successors added more violence than he intended but the principle of 'redemption' and its consequences have remained.

In the same way, the kibbutz, widely hailed as an attempt to create a Utopia, was and is an exclusivist Utopia; even if it is composed of atheists, it does not accept Arab members on principle and demands that potential members from other nationalities be first converted to Judaism. No wonder the kibbutz boys can be regarded as the most militaristic segment of the Israeli Jewish society.

It is this exclusivist ideology, rather than all the 'security needs' alleged by Israeli propaganda, which determines the takeovers of land in Israel in the 1950s and again in the mid-1960s and in the Occupied Territories after 1967. This ideology also dictated official Israeli plans for 'the Judaization of Galilee'. This curious term means encouraging Jews to settle in Galilee by giving them financial benefits. (I wonder what would be the reaction of US Jews if a plan for 'the Christianization of New York', or even only of Brooklyn, would be proposed in their country.) But the Redemption of the Land implies more than regional 'Judaization'. In the entire area of Israel the JNF, vigorously backed by Israeli state agencies (especially by the secret police) is spending great sums of public money in order to 'redeem' any land which non-Jews are willing to sell, and to preempt any attempt by a Jew to sell his land to a non-Jew by paying him a higher price.

Israeli Expansionism

The main danger which Israel, as 'a Jewish state', poses to its own people, to other Jews and to its neighbours, is its ideologically motivated pursuit of territorial expansion and the inevitable series of wars resulting from this aim. The more Israel becomes Jewish or, as one says in Hebrew, the more it 'returns to Judaism' (a process which has been under way in Israel at least since 1967), the more its actual politics are guided by Jewish ideological considerations and less by rational ones. My use of the term 'rational' does not refer here to a moral evaluation of Israeli policies, or to the supposed defence or security needs of Israel – even less so to the supposed needs of 'Israeli survival'. I am referring here to Israeli imperial policies based on its presumed interests. However morally bad or politically crass such policies are, I regard the adoption of policies based on 'Jewish ideology', in all its different versions as being even worse. The ideological defences of Israeli policies are usually based on Jewish religious beliefs or, in the case of secular Jews, on the 'historical rights' of the Jews, which derive from those beliefs and retain the dogmatic character of religious faith.

My own early political conversion from admirer of Ben-Gurion to his dedicated opponent began exactly with such an issue. In 1956 I eagerly swallowed all of Ben-Gurion's political and military reasons for Israel initiating the Suez War, until he (in spite of being an atheist, proud of his disregard of the commandments of Jewish religion) pronounced in the Knesset on the third day of that war, that the real reason for it is 'the restoration of the kingdom of David and Solomon' to its Biblical borders. At this point in his speech, almost every Knesset member spontaneously rose and sang the Israeli national anthem. To my knowledge, no zionist politician has ever repudiated Ben-Gurion's idea that Israeli policies must be based (within the limits of pragmatic considerations) on the restoration of the Biblical borders as the borders of the Jewish state. Indeed, close analysis of Israeli grand strategies and actual principles of foreign policy, as they are expressed in Hebrew, makes it clear that it is 'Jewish ideology', more than any other factor, which determines actual Israeli policies. The disregard of Judaism as it really is and of 'Jewish ideology' makes those policies incomprehensible to foreign observers who usually know nothing about Judaism except crude apologetics.

Let me give a more recent illustration of the essential difference which exists between Israeli imperial planning of the most inflated but secular type, and the principles of 'Jewish ideology'. The latter enjoins that land which was either ruled by any Jewish ruler in ancient times or was promised by God to the Jews, either in the Bible or – what is actually more important politically – according to a rabbinic interpretation of the Bible and the Talmud, should belong to Israel since it is a Jewish state. No doubt, many Jewish 'doves' are of the opinion that such conquest should be deferred to a time when Israel will be stronger than it is now, or that there would be, hopefully, 'a peaceful conquest', that is, that the Arab rulers or peoples would be 'persuaded' to cede the land in question in return for benefits which the Jewish state would then confer on them.

A number of discrepant versions of Biblical borders of the Land of Israel, which rabbinical authorities interpret as ideally belonging to the Jewish state, are in circulation. The most far-reaching among them include the following areas within these borders: in the south, all of Sinai and a part of northern Egypt up to the environs of Cairo; in the east, all of Jordan and a large chunk of Saudi Arabia, all of Kuwait and a part of Iraq south of the Euphrates; in the north, all of Lebanon and all of Syria together with a huge part of Turkey (up to lake Van); and in the west, Cyprus. An enormous body of research and learned discussion based on these borders, embodied in atlases, books, articles and more popular forms of propaganda is being published in Israel, often with state subsidies, or other forms of support. Certainly the late Kahane and his followers, as well as influential bodies such as Gush Emunim, not only desire the conquest of those territories by Israel, but regard it as a divinely commanded act, sure to be successful since it will be aided by God. In fact, important Jewish religious figures regard the Israeli refusal to undertake such a holy war, or even worse, the return of Sinai to Egypt, as a national sin which was justly punished by God. One of the more influential Gush Emunim rabbis, Dov Lior, the rabbi of Jewish settlements of Kiryat Arba and of Hebron, stated repeatedly that the Israeli failure to conquer Lebanon in 1982–5 was a well-merited divine punishment for its sin of 'giving a part of Land of Israel', namely Sinai, to Egypt.

Although I have chosen an admittedly extreme example of the Biblical borders of the Land of Israel which 'belong' to the 'Jewish state', those borders are quite popular in national–religious circles. There are less extreme versions of Biblical borders, sometimes also called 'historical borders'. It should however be emphasised that within Israel and the community of its diaspora Jewish supporters, the validity of the concept of either Biblical borders or historical borders as delineating the borders of land which belongs to Jews by right is not denied on grounds of principle, except by the tiny minority which opposes the concept of a Jewish state. Otherwise, objections to the realisation of such borders by a war are purely pragmatical. One can claim that Israel is now too weak to conquer all the land which 'belongs' to the Jews, or that the loss of Jewish lives (but not of Arab lives!) entailed in a war of conquest of such magnitude is more important than the conquest of the land, but in normative Judaism one cannot claim that 'the Land of Israel', in whatever borders, does not 'belong' to all the Jews. In May 1993, Ariel Sharon formally proposed in the Likud Convention that Israel should adopt the 'Biblical borders' concept as its official policy. There were rather few objections to this proposal, either in the Likud or outside it, and all were based on pragmatic grounds. No one even asked Sharon where exactly are the Biblical borders which he was urging that Israel should attain. Let us recall that among those who called themselves Leninists there was no doubt that history follows the principles laid out by Marx and Lenin. It is not only the belief itself, however dogmatic, but the refusal that it should ever be doubted, by thwarting open discussion, which creates a totalitarian cast of mind. Israeli-Jewish society and diaspora Jews who are leading 'Jewish lives' and organised in purely Jewish organisations, can be said therefore to have a strong streak of totalitarianism in their character.

However, an Israeli grand strategy, not based on the tenets of 'Jewish ideology', but based on purely strategic or imperial considerations had also developed since the inception of the state. An authoritative and lucid description of the principles governing such strategy was given by General (Reserves) Shlomo Gazit, a former Military Intelligence commander.[2] According to Gazit,

Israel's main task has not changed at all [since the demise of the USSR] and it remains of crucial importance. The geographical location of Israel at the centre of the Arab-Muslim Middle East predestines Israel to be a devoted guardian of stability in all the countries surrounding it. Its [role] is to protect the existing regimes: to prevent or halt the processes of radicalisation, and to block the expansion of fundamentalist religious zealotry.

For this purpose Israel will prevent changes occurring beyond Israel's borders [which it] will regard as intolerable, to the point of feeling compelled to use all its military power for the sake of their prevention or eradication.

In other words, Israel aims at imposing a hegemony on other Middle Eastern states. Needless to say, according to Gazit, Israel has a benevolent concern for the stability of Arab regimes. In Gazit's view, by protecting Middle Eastern regimes, Israel performs a vital service for 'the industrially advanced states, all of which are keenly concerned with guaranteeing the stability in the Middle East'. He argues that without Israel the existing regimes of the region would have collapsed long ago and that they remain in existence only because of Israeli threats. While this view may be hypocritical, one should recall in such contexts La Rochefoucault's maxim that 'hypocrisy is the tax which wickedness pays to virtue'. Redemption of the Land is an attempt to evade paying any such a tax.

Needless to say, I also oppose root and branch the Israeli non-ideological policies as they are so lucidly and correctly explained by Gazit. At the same time, I recognize that the dangers of the policies of Ben-Gurion or Sharon, motivated by 'Jewish ideology', are much worse than merely imperial policies, however criminal. The results of policies of other ideologically motivated regimes point in the same direction. The existence of an important component of Israeli policy, which is based on 'Jewish ideology' makes its analysis politically imperative. This ideology is, in turn, based on the attitudes of historic Judaism to non-Jews, one of the main themes of this book. Those attitudes necessarily influence many Jews, consciously or unconsciously. Our task here is to discuss historic Judaism in real terms.

The influence of 'Jewish ideology' on many Jews will be stronger the more it is hidden from public discussion. Such discussion will, it is hoped, lead people take the same attitude towards Jewish chauvinism and the contempt displayed by so many Jews towards non-Jews (which will be documented below) as that commonly taken towards antisemitism and all other forms of xenophobia, chauvinism and racism. It is justly assumed that only the full exposition, not only of antisemitism, but also of its historical roots, can be the basis of struggle against it. Likewise I am assuming that only the full exposition of Jewish chauvinism and religious fanaticism can be the basis of struggle against those phenomena. This is especially true today when, contrary to the situation prevailing fifty or sixty years ago, the political influence of Jewish chauvinism and religious fanaticism is much greater than that of antisemitism. But there is also another important consideration. I strongly believe that antisemitism and Jewish chauvinism can only be fought simultaneously.

A Closed Utopia?

Until such attitudes are widely adopted, the actual danger of Israeli policies based on 'Jewish ideology' remains greater than the danger of policies based on purely strategic considerations. The difference between the two kinds of policies was well expressed by Hugh Trevor-Roper in his essay 'Sir Thomas More and Utopia'[3] in which he termed them Platonic and Machiavellian:

> Machiavelli at least apologized for the methods which he thought necessary in politics. He regretted the necessity of force and fraud and did not call them by any other name. But Plato and More sanctified them, provided that they were used to sustain their own Utopian republics.

In a similar way true believers in that Utopia called the 'Jewish state', which will strive to achieve the 'Biblical borders', are more dangerous than the grand strategists of Gazit's type because their policies are being sanctified either by the use of religion or, worse, by the use of secularised religious principles which retain absolute validity. While Gazit at least sees a need to argue that the Israeli diktat benefits the Arab regimes, Ben-Gurion did not pretend that the re-establishment of the kingdom of David and Solomon will benefit anybody except the Jewish state.

Using the concepts of Platonism to analyse Israeli policies based on 'Jewish ideology' should not seem strange. It was noticed by several scholars, of whom the most important was Moses Hadas, who claimed that the foundations of 'classical Judaism', that is, of Judaism as it was established by talmudic sages, are based on Platonic influences and especially on the image of Sparta as it appears in Plato.[4] According to Hadas, a crucial feature of the Platonic political system, adopted by Judaism as early as the Maccabean period (142–63 BC), was 'that every phase of human conduct be subjected to religious sanctions which are in fact to be manipulated by the ruler'. There can be no better definition of 'classical Judaism' and of the ways in which the rabbis manipulated it than this Platonic definition. In particular, Hadas claims that Judaism adopted what 'Plato himself summarized [as] the objectives of his program', in the following well-known passage:

> The principal thing is that no one, man or woman, should ever be without an officer set over him, and that none should get the mental habit of taking any step, whether in earnest or in jest, on his individual responsibility. In peace as in war he must live always with his eyes on his superior officer ... In a word, we must train the mind not even to consider acting as an individual or know how to do it. (*Laws*, 942 ab)

If the word 'rabbi' is substituted for 'an officer' we will have a perfect image of classical Judaism. The latter is still deeply influencing Israeli-Jewish society and determining to a large extent the Israeli policies.

It was the above quoted passage which was chosen by Karl Popper in *The Open Society and Its Enemies* as describing the essence of 'a closed society'. Historical Judaism and its two successors, Jewish Orthodoxy and Zionism, are both sworn enemies of the concept of the open society as applied to Israel. A Jewish state, whether based on its present Jewish ideology or, if it becomes even more Jewish in character than it is now, on the principles of Jewish Orthodoxy, cannot ever contain an open society. There are two choices which face Israeli-Jewish society. It can become a fully closed and warlike ghetto, a Jewish Sparta, supported by the labour of Arab helots, kept in existence by its influence on the US political establishment and by threats to use its nuclear power, or it can try to become an open society. The second choice is dependent on a honest examination of its Jewish past, on the admission that Jewish chauvinism and exclusivism exist, and on a honest examination of the attitudes of Judaism towards the non-Jews.

Chapter 2

Prejudice and Prevarication

The first difficulty in writing about this subject is that the term 'Jew' has been used during the last 150 years with two rather different meanings. To understand this, let us imagine ourselves in the year 1780. Then the universally accepted meaning of the term 'Jew' basically coincided with what the Jews themselves understood as constituting their own identity. This identity was primarily religious, but the precepts of religion governed the details of daily behaviour in all aspects of life, both social and private, among the Jews themselves as well as in their relation to non-Jews. It was then literally true that a Jew could not even drink a glass of water in the home of a non-Jew. And the same basic laws of behaviour towards non-Jews were equally valid from Yemen to New York. Whatever the term by which the Jews of 1780 may be described – and I do not wish to enter into a metaphysical dispute about terms like, 'nation' and 'people'[1] – it is clear that all Jewish communities at that time were separate from the non-Jewish societies in the midst of which they were living.

However, all this was changed by two parallel processes – beginning in Holland and England, continuing in revolutionary France and in countries which followed the example of the French Revolution, and then in the modern monarchies of the 19th century: the Jews gained a significant level of individual rights (in some cases full legal equality), and the legal power of the Jewish community over its members was destroyed. It should be noted that both developments were simultaneous, and that the latter is even more important, albeit less widely known, than the former.

Since the time of the late Roman Empire, Jewish communities had considerable legal powers over their members. Not only powers which arise through voluntary mobilisation of social pressure (for example refusal to have any dealing whatsoever with an excommunicated Jew or even to bury his body), but a power of naked coercion: to flog, to imprison, to expel – all this could be inflicted quite legally on an individual Jew by the rabbinical courts for all kinds of offences. In many countries – Spain and Poland are notable examples – even capital punishment could be and was inflicted, sometimes using particularly cruel methods such as flogging to death. All this was not only permitted but positively encouraged by the state authorities in both Christian and Muslim countries, who besides their general interest in preserving 'law and order' had in some cases a more direct financial interest as well. For example, in Spanish archives dating from the 13th and 14th centuries there are records of many detailed orders issued by those most devout Catholic Kings of Castile and Aragon, instructing their no less devout officials to co-operate with the rabbis in enforcing observance of the Sabbath by the Jews. Why? Because whenever a Jew was fined by a rabbinical court for violating the Sabbath, the rabbis had to hand nine tenths of the fine over to the king – a very profitable and effective arrangement. Similarly, one can quote from the *responsa* written shortly before 1832 by the famous Rabbi Moshe Sofer of Pressburg (now Bratislava), in what was then the autonomous Hungarian Kingdom in the Austrian Empire, and addressed to Vienna in Austria proper, where the Jews had already been granted some considerable individual rights.[2] He laments the fact that since the Jewish congregation in Vienna lost its powers to punish offenders, the Jews there have become lax in matters of religious observance, and adds: 'Here in Pressburg, when I am told that a Jewish shopkeeper dared to open his shop during the Lesser Holidays, I immediately send a policeman to imprison him.'

This was the most important social fact of Jewish existence before the advent of the modern state: observance of the religious laws of Judaism, as well as their inculcation through education, were enforced on Jews by physical coercion, from which one could only escape by conversion to the religion of the majority, amounting in the circumstances to a total social break and for that reason very impracticable, except during a religious crisis.[3]

However, once the modern state had come into existence, the Jewish community lost its powers to punish or intimidate the individual Jew. The bonds of one of the most closed of 'closed societies', one of the most totalitarian societies in the whole history of mankind were snapped. This act of liberation came mostly from *outside*; although there were some Jews who helped it from within, these were at first very few. This form of liberation had very grave consequences for the future. Just as in the case of Germany (according to the masterly analysis of A.J.P. Taylor) it was easy to ally the cause of reaction with patriotism, because in actual fact individual rights and equality before the law were brought into Germany by the armies of the French Revolution and of Napoleon, and one could brand liberty as 'un-German', exactly so it turned out to be very easy among the Jews, particularly in Israel, to mount a very effective attack against all the notions and ideals of humanism and the rule of law (not to say democracy) as something 'un-Jewish' or 'anti-Jewish' – as indeed they are, *in a historical sense* – and as principles which may be used in the 'Jewish interest', but which have no validity *against* the 'Jewish interest', for example when Arabs invoke these same principles. This has also led – again just as in Germany and other nations of *Mitteleuropa* – to a deceitful, sentimental and ultra-romantic Jewish historiography, from which all inconvenient facts have been expunged.

So one will not find in Hannah Arendt's voluminous writings, whether on totalitarianism or on Jews, or on both,[4] the smallest hint as to what Jewish society in Germany was really like in the 18th century: burning of books, persecution of writers, disputes about the magic powers of amulets, bans on the most elementary 'non-Jewish' education such as the teaching of correct German or indeed German written in the Latin alphabet.[5] Nor can one find in the numerous English-language 'Jewish histories' the elementary facts about the attitude of Jewish mysticism (so fashionable at present in certain quarters) to non-Jews: that they are considered to be, literally, limbs of Satan, and that the few non-satanic individuals among them (that is, those who convert to Judaism) are in reality 'Jewish souls' who got lost when Satan violated the Holy Lady (*Shekhinah* or Matronit, one of the female components of the Godhead, sister and wife of the younger male God according to the cabbala) in her heavenly abode. The great authorities, such as Gershom Scholem, have lent their authority to a system of deceptions in all the 'sensitive' areas, the more popular ones being the most dishonest and misleading.

But the social consequence of this process of liberalisation was that, for the first time since about AD 200,[6] a Jew could be free to do what he liked, within the bounds of his country's civil law, without having to pay for this freedom by converting to another religion. The freedom to learn and read books in modern languages, the freedom to read and write books in Hebrew not approved by the rabbis (as any Hebrew or Yiddish book previously had to be), the freedom to eat non-kosher food, the freedom to ignore the numerous absurd taboos regulating sexual life, even the freedom to think – for 'forbidden thoughts' are among the most serious sins – all these were granted to the Jews of Europe (and subsequently of other countries) by modern or even absolutist European regimes, although the latter were at the same time antisemitic and oppressive. Nicholas I of Russia was a notorious antisemite and issued many laws against the Jews of his state. But he also strengthened the forces of 'law and order' in

Russia – not only the secret police but also the regular police and the gendarmerie – with the consequence that it became difficult to murder Jews on the order of their rabbis, whereas in pre-1795 Poland it had been quite easy. 'Official' Jewish history condemns him on *both* counts. For example, in the late 1830s a 'Holy Rabbi' (*Tzadik*) in a small Jewish town in the Ukraine ordered the murder of a heretic by throwing him into the boiling water of the town baths, and contemporary Jewish sources note with astonishment and horror that bribery was 'no longer effective' and that not only the actual perpetrators but also the Holy Man were severely punished. The Metternich regime of pre-1848 Austria was notoriously reactionary and quite unfriendly to Jews, but it did not allow people, even liberal Jewish rabbis, to be poisoned. During 1848, when the regime's power was temporarily weakened, the first thing the leaders of the Jewish community in the Galician city of Lemberg (now Lvov) did with their newly regained freedom was to poison the liberal rabbi of the city, whom the tiny non-Orthodox Jewish group in the city had imported from Germany. One of his greatest heresies, by the way, was the advocacy and actual performance of the Bar Mitzvah ceremony, which had recently been invented.

Liberation from Outside

In the last 150 years, the term 'Jew' has therefore acquired a dual meaning, to the great confusion of some well-meaning people, particularly in the English-speaking countries, who imagine that the Jews they meet socially are 'representative' of Jews 'in general'. In the countries of east Europe as well as in the Arab world, the Jews were liberated from the tyranny of their own religion and of their own communities *by outside forces*, too late and in circumstances too unfavourable for genuine internalised social change. In most cases, and particularly in Israel, the old concept of society, the same ideology – especially as directed towards non-Jews – and the same utterly false conception of history have been preserved. This applies even to some of those Jews who joined 'progressive' or leftist movements. An examination of radical, socialist and communist parties can provide many examples of disguised Jewish chauvinists and racists, who joined these parties merely for reasons of 'Jewish interest' and are, in Israel, in favour of 'anti-Gentile' discrimination. One need only check how many Jewish 'socialists' have managed to write about the kibbutz without taking the trouble to mention that it is a racist institution from which non-Jewish citizens of Israel are rigorously excluded, to see that

the phenomenon we are alluding to is by no means uncommon.[7]

Avoiding labels based on ignorance or hypocrisy, we thus
see that the word 'Jewry' and its cognates describe *two different
and even contrasting social groups*, and because of current Israeli
politics the continuum between the two is disappearing fast. On
the one hand there is the traditional totalitarian meaning discussed above; on the other hand there are Jews by descent
who have internalised the complex of ideas which Karl Popper
has called 'the open society'. (There are also some, particularly
in the USA, who have not internalised these ideas, but try to
make a show of acceptance.)

It is important to note that *all* the supposedly 'Jewish
characteristics' - by which I mean the traits which vulgar
so-called intellectuals in the West attribute to 'the Jews' - are
modern characteristics, quite unknown during most of Jewish
history, and appeared only when the totalitarian Jewish community began to lose its power. Take, for example, the
famous Jewish sense of humour. Not only is humour very
rare in Hebrew literature before the 19th century (and is
only found during few periods, in countries where the Jewish
upper class was relatively free from the rabbinical yoke, such
as Italy between the 14th and 17th centuries or Muslim
Spain) but humour and jokes are strictly forbidden by the
Jewish religion - except, significantly, jokes against other religions. Satire against rabbis and leaders of the community was
never internalised by Judaism, not even to a small extent, as
it was in Latin Christianity. There were no Jewish comedies,
just as there were no comedies in Sparta, and for a similar
reason.[8] Or take the love of learning. Except for a purely
religious learning, which was itself in a debased and degenerate state, the Jews of Europe (and to a somewhat lesser
extent also of the Arab countries) were dominated, before
about 1780, by a supreme contempt and hate for all learning
(excluding the Talmud and Jewish mysticism). Large parts of
the Old Testament, all non-liturgical Hebrew poetry, most
books on Jewish philosophy were not read and their very
names were often anathematised. Study of all languages was
strictly forbidden, as was the study of mathematics and science. Geography,[9] history - even Jewish history - were completely unknown. The critical sense, which is supposedly so
characteristic of Jews, was totally absent, and nothing was so
forbidden, feared and therefore persecuted as the most mod-
est innovation or the most innocent criticism.

It was a world sunk in the most abject superstition, fanaticism and ignorance, a world in which the preface to the first

work on geography in Hebrew (published in 1803 in Russia) could complain that very many great rabbis were denying the existence of the American continent and saying that it is 'impossible'. Between that world and what is often taken in the West to 'characterise' Jews there is nothing in common except the mistaken name.

However, a great many present-day Jews are nostalgic for that world, their lost paradise, the comfortable closed society from which they were not so much liberated as expelled. A large part of the zionist movement always wanted to restore it – and this part has gained the upper hand. Many of the motives behind Israeli politics, which so bewilder the poor confused western 'friends of Israel', are perfectly explicable once they are seen simply as reaction, reaction in the political sense which this word has had for the last two hundred years: a forced and in many respects innovative, and therefore illusory, return to the closed society of the Jewish past.

Obstacles to Understanding

Historically it can be shown that a closed society is not interested in a description of itself, no doubt because any description is in part a form of critical analysis and so may encourage critical 'forbidden thoughts'. The more a society becomes open, the more it is interested in reflecting, at first descriptively and then critically, upon itself, its present working as well as its past. But what happens when a faction of intellectuals desires to drag a society, which has already opened up to a considerable extent, back to its previous totalitarian, closed condition? Then the very means of the former progress – philosophy, the sciences, history and especially sociology – become the most effective instruments of the 'treason of the intellectuals'. They are perverted in order to serve as devices of deception, and in the process they degenerate.

Classical Judaism [10] had little interest in describing or explaining itself to the members of its own community, whether educated (in talmudic studies) or not.[11] It is significant that the writing of Jewish history, even in the driest annalistic style, ceased completely from the time of Josephus Flavius (end of first century) until the Renaissance, when it was revived for a short time in Italy and in other countries where the Jews were under strong Italian influence.[12] Characteristically, the rabbis feared Jewish even more than general history, and the first modern book on history published in Hebrew (in the 16th century) was entitled *History of the Kings of France and of the Ottoman Kings*. It was followed by some histories dealing only with the persecutions that

Jews had been subjected to. The first book on Jewish history proper[13] (dealing with ancient times) was promptly banned and suppressed by the highest rabbinical authorities, and did not reappear before the 19th century. The rabbinical authorities of east Europe furthermore decreed that all non-talmudic studies are to be forbidden, even when nothing specific could be found in them which merits anathema, because they encroach on the time that should be employed either in studying the Talmud or in making money – which should be used to subsidise talmudic scholars. Only one loophole was left, namely the time that even a pious Jew must perforce spend in the privy. In that unclean place sacred studies are forbidden, and it was therefore permitted to read history there, provided it was written in Hebrew and was completely secular, which in effect meant that it must be exclusively devoted to non-Jewish subjects. (One can imagine that those few Jews of that time who – no doubt tempted by Satan – developed an interest in the history of the French kings were constantly complaining to their neighbours about the constipation they were suffering from ...) As a consequence, two hundred years ago the vast majority of Jews were totally in the dark not only about the existence of America but also about Jewish history and Jewry's contemporary state; and they were quite content to remain so.

A Totalitarian History

There was however one area in which they were not allowed to remain self-contented – the area of Christian attacks against those passages in the Talmud and the talmudic literature which are specifically anti-Christian or more generally anti-Gentile. It is important to note that this challenge developed relatively late in the history of Christian–Jewish relations – only from the 13th century on. (Before that time, the Christian authorities attacked Judaism using either Biblical or general arguments, but seemed to be quite ignorant as to the contents of the Talmud.) The Christian campaign against the Talmud was apparently brought on by the conversion to Christianity of Jews who were well versed in the Talmud and who were in many cases attracted by the development of Christian philosophy, with its strong Aristotelian (and thus universal) character.[14]

It must be admitted at the outset that the Talmud and the talmudic literature – quite apart from the general anti-Gentile streak that runs through them, which will be discussed in greater detail in Chapter 5 – contain very offensive statements and precepts directed specifically against Christianity. For example, in addition to a series of scurrilous sexual allegations against Jesus, the Talmud states that his punishment in hell is to be immersed in boiling excrement – a statement not exactly calculated to endear the Talmud to devout Christians. Or one can quote the precept according to which Jews are instructed to burn, publicly if possible, any copy of the New Testament that comes into their hands. (This is not only still in force but actually practised today; thus on 23 March 1980 hundreds of copies of the New Testament were publicly and ceremonially burnt in Jerusalem under the auspices of Yad Le'akhim, a Jewish religious organisation subsidised by the Israeli Ministry of Religions.)

Anyway, a powerful attack, well based in many points, against talmudic Judaism developed in Europe from the 13th century. We are not referring here to ignorant calumnies, such as the blood libel, propagated by benighted monks in small provincial cities, but to serious disputations held before the best European universities of the time and on the whole conducted as fairly as was possible under medieval circumstances.[15]

What was the Jewish – or rather the rabbinical – response? The simplest one was the ancient weapon of bribery and string-pulling. In most European countries, during most of the time, anything could be fixed by a bribe. Nowhere was this maxim more true than in the Rome of the Renaissance popes. The *Editio Princeps* of the complete Code of Talmudic Law, Maimonides' *Mishneh Torah* – replete not only with the most offensive precepts against all Gentiles but also with explicit attacks on Christianity and on Jesus (after whose name the author adds piously, 'May the name of the wicked perish') – was published unexpurgated in Rome in the year 1480 under Sixtus IV, politically a very active pope who had a constant and urgent need for money. (A few years earlier, the only older edition of *The Golden Ass* by Apuleius from which the violent attack on Christianity had not been removed was also published in Rome.) Alexander VI Borgia was also very liberal in this respect.

Even during that period, as well as before it, there were always countries in which for a time a wave of anti-Talmud persecution set in. But a more consistent and widespread onslaught came with the Reformation and Counter Reformation, which induced a higher standard of intellectual honesty as well as a better knowledge of Hebrew among Christian scholars. From the 16th century, all the talmudic literature, including the Talmud itself, was subjected to Christian censorship in various countries. In Russia this went on until 1917. Some censors, such as in Holland, were more lax, while others were more severe; and the offensive passages were expunged or modified.

All modern studies on Judaism, particularly by Jews, have evolved from that conflict, and to this day they bear the unmistakable marks of their origin: deception, apologetics or hostile polemics, indifference or even active hostility to the pursuit of truth. Almost all the so-called *Jewish studies in Judaism*, from that time to this very day, are polemics against an external enemy rather than an internal debate.

It is important to note that this was initially the character of historiography in all known societies (except ancient Greece, whose early liberal historians were attacked by later sophists for their insufficient patriotism!). This was true of the early Catholic and Protestant historians, who polemicised against each other. Similarly, the earliest European national histories are imbued with the crudest nationalism and scorn for all other, neighbouring nations. But sooner or later there comes a time when an attempt is made to understand one's national or religious adversary and at the same time to criticise certain deep and important aspects of the history of one's own group; and both these developments go together. Only when historiography becomes – as Pieter Geyl put it so well – 'a debate without end' rather than a continuation of war by historiographic means, only then does a humane historiography, which strives for both accuracy and fairness, become possible; and it then turns into one of the most powerful instruments of humanism and self-education.

It is for this reason that modern totalitarian regimes rewrite history or punish historians.[16] When a whole society tries to return to totalitarianism, a totalitarian history is written, not because of compulsion from above but under pressure from below, which is much more effective. This is what happened in Jewish history, and this constitutes the first obstacle we have to surmount.

Defence Mechanisms

What were the detailed mechanisms (other than bribery) employed by Jewish communities, in cooperation with outside forces, in order to ward off the attack on the Talmud and other religious literature? Several methods can be distinguished, all of them having important political consequences reflected in current Israeli policies. Although it would be tedious to supply in each case the Beginistic or Labour-zionist parallel, I am sure that readers who are somewhat familiar with the details of Middle East politics will themselves be able to notice the resemblance.

The first mechanism I shall discuss is that of *surreptitious defiance, combined with outward compliance*. As explained above, talmudic passages directed against Christianity or against non-Jews[17] had to go or to be modified – the pressure was too strong. This is what was done: a few of the most offensive passages were bodily removed from all editions printed in Europe after the mid-16th century. In all other passages, the expressions 'Gentile', 'non-Jew', 'stranger' (goy, eino yehudi, nokhri) – which appear in all early manuscripts and printings as well as in all editions published in Islamic countries – were replaced by terms such as 'idolator', 'heathen' or even 'Canaanite' or 'Samaritan', terms which could be explained away but which a Jewish reader could recognise as euphemisms for the old expressions.

As the attack mounted, so the defence became more elaborate, sometimes with lasting tragic results. During certain periods the Tsarist Russian censorship became stricter and, seeing the above mentioned euphemisms for what they were, forbade them too. Thereupon the rabbinical authorities substituted the terms 'Arab' or 'Muslim' (in Hebrew, Yishma'eli – which means both) or occasionally 'Egyptian', correctly calculating that the Tsarist authorities would not object to this kind of abuse. At the same time, lists of Talmudic Omissions were circulated in manuscript form, which explained all the new terms and pointed out all the omissions. At times, a general disclaimer was printed before the title page of each volume of talmudic literature, solemnly declaring, sometimes on oath, that all hostile expressions in that volume are intended only against the idolators of antiquity, or even against the long-vanished Canaanites, rather than against 'the peoples in whose land we live'. After the British conquest of India, some rabbis hit on the subterfuge of claiming that any particularly outrageous derogatory expression used by them is only intended against the Indians. Occasionally the aborigines of Australia were also added as whipping-boys.

Needless to say, all this was a calculated lie from beginning to end; and following the establishment of the State of Israel, once the rabbis felt secure, all the offensive passages and expressions were restored without hesitation in all new editions. (Because of the enormous cost which a new edition involves, a considerable part of the talmudic literature, including the Talmud itself, is still being reprinted from the old editions. For this reason, the above mentioned Talmudic Omissions have now been published in Israel in a cheap printed edition, under the title Hesronot Shas.) So now one can read quite freely – and Jewish children are actually taught – passages such as that[18] which commands every Jew, whenever passing near a cemetery, to utter a blessing if the cemetery is Jewish, but to curse the

mothers of the dead[19] if it is non-Jewish. In the old editions
the curse was omitted, or one of the euphemisms was substituted for 'Gentiles'. But in the new Israeli edition of Rabbi
Adin Steinsalz (complete with Hebrew explanations and glosses
to the Aramaic parts of the text, so that schoolchildren should
be in no doubt as to what they are supposed to say) the
unambiguous words 'Gentiles' and 'strangers' have been restored.

Under external pressure, the rabbis deceptively eliminated or
modified certain passages – but not the actual practices which
are prescribed in them. It is a fact which must be remembered,
not least by Jews themselves, that for centuries our totalitarian
society has employed barbaric and inhumane customs to poison
the minds of its members, and it is still doing so. (These
inhumane customs cannot be explained away as mere reaction
to antisemitism or persecution of Jews; they are gratuitous
barbarities directed against each and every human being. A
pious Jew arriving for the first time in Australia, say, and
chancing to pass near an Aboriginal graveyard, must – as an
act of worship of 'God' – curse the mothers of the dead buried
there.) Without facing this real social fact, we all become
parties to the deception and accomplices to the process of
poisoning the present and future generations, with all the consequences of this process.

The Deception Continues

Modern scholars of Judaism have not only continued the deception, but have actually improved upon the old rabbinical methods,
both in impudence and in mendacity. I omit here the various
histories of antisemitism, as unworthy of serious consideration,
and shall give just three particular examples and one general
example of the more modern 'scholarly' deceptions.

In 1962, a part of the Maimonidean Code referred to
above, the so-called Book of Knowledge, which contains the
most basic rules of Jewish faith and practice, was published in
Jerusalem in a bilingual edition, with the English translation
facing the Hebrew text.[20] The latter has been restored to its
original purity, and the command to exterminate Jewish infidels
appears in it in full: 'It is a duty to exterminate them with
one's own hands.' In the English translation this is somewhat
softened to: 'It is a duty to take active measures to destroy
them.' But then the Hebrew text goes on to specify the prime
examples of 'infidels' who must be exterminated: 'Such as Jesus
of Nazareth and his pupils, and Tzadoq and Baitos[21] and their
pupils, may the name of the wicked rot'. *Not one word* of this

appears in the English text on the facing page (78a). And, even more significant, in spite of the wide circulation of this book among scholars in the English-speaking countries, not one of them has, as far as I know, protested against this glaring deception.

The second example comes from the USA, again from an English translation of a book by Maimonides. Apart from his work on the codification of the Talmud, he was also a philosopher and his *Guide to the Perplexed* is justly considered to be the greatest work of Jewish religious philosophy and is widely read and used even today. Unfortunately, in addition to his attitude towards non-Jews generally and Christians in particular, Maimonides was also an anti-Black racist. Towards the end of the *Guide*, in a crucial chapter (book III, chapter 51) he discusses how various sections of humanity can attain the supreme religious value, the true worship of God. Among those who are incapable of even approaching this are:

> Some of the Turks [i.e., the Mongol race] and the nomads in the North, and the Blacks and the nomads in the South, and those who resemble them in our climates. And their nature is like the nature of mute animals, and according to my opinion they are not on the level of human beings, and their level among existing things is below that of a man and above that of a monkey, because they have the image and the resemblance of a man more than a monkey does.

Now, what does one do with such a passage in a most important and *necessary* work of Judaism? Face the truth and its consequences? God forbid! Admit (as so many Christian scholars, for example, have done in similar circumstances) that a very important Jewish authority held also rabid anti-Black views, and by this admission make an attempt at self-education in real humanity? Perish the thought. I can almost imagine Jewish scholars in the USA consulting among themselves, 'What is to be done?' – for the book *had* to be translated, due to the decline in the knowledge of Hebrew among American Jews. Whether by consultation or by individual inspiration, a happy 'solution' was found: in the popular American translation of the *Guide* by one Friedlander, first published as far back as 1925 and since then reprinted in many editions, including several in paperback, the Hebrew word *Kushim*, which means Blacks, was simply transliterated and appears as 'Kushites', a word which means nothing to those who have no knowledge of Hebrew, or to whom an obliging rabbi will not give an *oral* explanation.[22] During all these years, not a word has been said to point out the initial deception or the social facts underlying its continuation – and this throughout the excitement of Martin Luther King's campaigns, which were supported by so many rabbis, not to mention other Jewish figures, some of whom must have been aware of the anti-Black racist attitude which forms part of their Jewish heritage.[23]

Surely one is driven to the hypothesis that quite a few of Martin Luther King's rabbinical supporters were either anti-Black racists who supported him for tactical reasons of 'Jewish interest' (wishing to win Black support for American Jewry and for Israel's policies) or were accomplished hypocrites, to the point of schizophrenia, capable of passing very rapidly from a hidden enjoyment of rabid racism to a proclaimed attachment to an anti-racist struggle – and back – and back again.

The third example comes from a work which has far less serious scholarly intent – but is all the more popular for that: *The Joys of Yiddish* by Leo Rosten. This light-hearted work – first published in the USA in 1968, and reprinted in many editions, including several times as a Penguin paperback – is a kind of glossary of Yiddish words often used by Jews or even non-Jews in English-speaking countries. For each entry, in addition to a detailed definition and more or less amusing anecdotes illustrating its use, there is also an etymology stating (quite accurately, on the whole) the language from which the word came into Yiddish and its meaning in that language. The entry *Shaygets* – whose main meaning is 'a Gentile boy or young man' – is an exception: there the etymology cryptically states 'Hebrew origin', without giving the form or meaning of the original Hebrew word. However, under the entry *Shiksa* – the feminine form of *Shaygets* – the author does give the original Hebrew word, *sheqetz* (or, in his transliteration, *sheques*) and defines its Hebrew meaning as 'blemish'. This is a bare-faced lie, as every speaker of Hebrew knows. The *Megiddo Modern Hebrew–English Dictionary*, published in Israel, correctly defines *sheqetz* as follows: 'unclean animal; loathsome creature, abomination (colloquial – pronounced shaygets) wretch, unruly youngster; Gentile youngster'.

My final, more general example is, if possible, even more shocking than the others. It concerns the attitude of the Hassidic movement towards non-Jews. Hassidism – a continuation (and debasement!) of Jewish mysticism – is still a *living* movement, with hundreds of thousands of active adherents who are fanatically devoted to their 'holy rabbis', some of whom have acquired a very considerable political influence in Israel, among the leaders of most parties and even more so in the higher echelons of the army.

What, then, are the views of this movement concerning

non-Jews? As an example, let us take the famous *Hatanya*, fundamental book of the Habbad movement, one of the most important branches of Hassidism. According to this book, all non-Jews are totally satanic creatures 'in whom there is absolutely nothing good'. Even a non-Jewish embryo is qualitatively different from a Jewish one. The very existence of a non-Jew is 'inessential', whereas all of creation was created solely for the sake of the Jews.

This book is circulated in countless editions, and its ideas are further propagated in the numerous 'discourses' of the present hereditary Fuehrer of Habbad, the so-called Lubavitcher rabbi, M.M. Schneurssohn, who leads this powerful world-wide organisation from his New York headquarters. In Israel these ideas are widely disseminated among the public at large, in the schools and in the army. (According to the testimony of Shulamit Aloni, Member of the Knesset, this Habbad propaganda was particularly stepped up before Israel's invasion of Lebanon in March 1978, in order to induce military doctors and nurses to withhold medical help from 'Gentile wounded'. This Nazi-like advice did not refer specifically to Arabs or Palestinians, but simply to 'Gentiles', *goyim*.) A former Israeli President, Shazar, was an ardent adherent of Habbad, and many top Israeli and American politicians – headed by Prime Minister Begin – publicly courted and supported it. This, in spite of the considerable unpopularity of the Lubavitcher rabbi – in Israel he is widely criticised because he refuses to come to the Holy Land even for a visit and keeps himself in New York for obscure messianic reasons, while in New York his anti-Black attitude is notorious.

The fact that, *despite* these pragmatic difficulties, Habbad can be publicly supported by so many top political figures owes much to the thoroughly disingenuous and misleading treatment by almost all scholars who have written about the Hassidic movement and its Habbad branch. This applies particularly to all who have written or are writing about it in English. They suppress the glaring evidence of the old Hassidic texts as well as the latter-day political implications that follow from them, which stare in the face of even a casual reader of the Israeli Hebrew press, in whose pages the Lubavitcher rabbi and other Hassidic leaders constantly publish the most rabid bloodthirsty statements and exhortations against all Arabs.

A chief deceiver in this case, and a good example of the power of the deception, was Martin Buber. His numerous works eulogising the whole Hassidic movement (including Habbad) never so much as hint at the real doctrines of Hassidism concerning non-Jews. The crime of deception is all the greater in view of the fact that Buber's eulogies of Hassidism were first published in German during the period of the rise of German nationalism and the accession of Nazism to power. But while ostensibly opposing Nazism, Buber glorified a movement holding and actually teaching doctrines about non-Jews not unlike the Nazi doctrines about Jews. One could of course argue that the Hassidic Jews of seventy or fifty years ago were the victims, and a 'white lie' favouring a victim is excusable. But the consequences of deception are incalculable. Buber's works were translated into Hebrew, were made a powerful element of the Hebrew education in Israel, have greatly increased the power of the bloodthirsty Hassidic leaders, and have thus been an important factor in the rise of Israeli chauvinism and hate of all non-Jews. If we think about the many human beings who died of their wounds because Israeli army nurses, incited by Hassidic propaganda, refused to tend them, then a heavy onus for their blood lies on the head of Martin Buber.

I must mention here that in his adulation of Hassidism Buber far surpassed other Jewish scholars, particularly those writing in Hebrew (or, formerly, in Yiddish) or even in European languages but purely for a Jewish audience. In questions of internal Jewish interest, there had once been a great deal of justified criticism of the Hassidic movement. Their mysogynism (much more extreme than that common to all Jewish Orthodoxy), their indulgence in alcohol, their fanatical cult of their hereditary 'holy rabbis' who extorted money from them, the numerous superstitions peculiar to them – these and many other negative traits were critically commented upon. But Buber's sentimental and deceitful romantisation has won the day, especially in the USA and Israel, because it was in tune with the totalitarian admiration of anything 'genuinely Jewish' and because certain 'left' Jewish circles in which Buber had a particularly great influence have adopted this position.

Nor was Buber alone in his attitude, although in my opinion he was by far the worst in the evil he propagated and the influence he has left behind him. There was the very influential sociologist and biblical scholar, Yehezkiel Kaufman, an advocate of genocide on the model of the Book of Joshua, the idealist philosopher Hugo Shmuel Bergman, who as far back as 1914–15 advocated the expulsion of all Palestinians to Iraq, and many others. All were outwardly 'dovish', but employed formulas which could be manipulated in the most extreme anti-Arab sense, all had tendencies to that religious mysticism which encourages the propagation of deceptions, and all seemed to be gentle persons who, even when advocating expulsion, racism and genocide, seemed incapable of hurting a fly – and just for this reason the effect of their deceptions was the greater.

It is against the glorification of inhumanity, proclaimed not only by the rabbis but by those who are supposed to be the greatest and certainly the most influential scholars of Judaism, that we have to struggle; and it is against those modern successors of the false prophets and dishonest priests that we have to repeat – even in the face of an almost unanimous opinion within Israel and among the majority of Jews in countries such as the USA – Lucretius' warning against surrendering one's judgement to the declamations of religious leaders: *Tantum religio potuit suadere malorum* – 'To such heights of evil are men driven by religion.' Religion is not always (as Marx said) the opium of the people, but it can often be so, and when it is used in this sense by prevaricating and misrepresenting its true nature, the scholars and intellectuals who perform this task take on the character of opium smugglers.

But we can derive from this analysis another, more general conclusion about the most effective and horrific means of compulsion to do evil, to cheat and to deceive and, while keeping one's hands quite clean of violence, to corrupt whole peoples and drive them to oppression and murder. (For there can no longer be any doubt that the most horrifying acts of oppression in the West Bank are motivated by Jewish religious fanaticism.) Most people seem to assume that the worst totalitarianism employs physical coercion, and would refer to the imagery of Orwell's *1984* for a model illustrating such a regime. But it seems to me that this common view is greatly mistaken, and that the intuition of Isaac Asimov, in whose science fiction the worst oppression is always internalised, is the more true to the dangers of human nature. Unlike Stalin's tame scholars, the rabbis – and even more so the scholars attacked here, and with them the whole mob of equally silent middlebrows such as writers, journalists, public figures, who lie and deceive more than them – are not facing the danger of death or concentration camp, but only social pressure; they lie out of patriotism because they believe that it is their duty to lie for what they conceive to be the Jewish interest. They are *patriotic liars*, and it is the same patriotism which reduces them to silence when confronted with the discrimination and oppression of the Palestinians.

In the present case we are also faced with another group loyalty, but one which comes from outside the group, and which is sometimes even more mischievous. Very many non-

Jews (including Christian clergy and religious laymen, as well as some marxists from all marxist groups) hold the curious opinion that one way to 'atone' for the persecution of Jews is not to speak out against evil perpetrated by Jews but to participate in 'white lies' about them. The crude accusation of 'antisemitism' (or, in the case of Jews, 'self-hate') against anybody who protests at the discrimination of Palestinians or who points out any fact about the Jewish religion or the Jewish past which conflicts with the 'approved version' comes with greater hostility and force from non-Jewish 'friends of the Jews' than from Jews. It is the existence and great influence of this group in all western countries, and particularly in the USA (as well as the other English-speaking countries) which has allowed the rabbis and scholars of Judaism to propagate their lies not only without opposition but with considerable help.

In fact, many professed 'anti-stalinists' have merely substituted another idol for their worship, and tend to support Jewish racism and fanaticism with even greater ardour and dishonesty than were found among the most devoted stalinists in the past. Although this phenomenon of blind and stalinistic support for any evil, so long as it is 'Jewish', is particularly strong from 1945, when the truth about the extermination of European Jewry became known, it is a mistake to suppose that it began only then. On the contrary, it dates very far back, particularly in social-democratic circles. One of Marx's early friends, Moses Hess, widely known and respected as one of the first socialists in Germany, subsequently revealed himself as an extreme Jewish racist, whose views about the 'pure Jewish race' published in 1858 were not unlike comparable bilge about the 'pure Aryan race'. But the German socialists, who struggled against German racism, remained silent about their Jewish racism.

In 1944, during the actual struggle against Hitler, the British Labour Party approved a plan for the expulsion of Palestinians from Palestine, which was similar to Hitler's early plans (up to about 1941) for the Jews. This plan was approved under the pressure of Jewish members of the party's leadership, many of whom have displayed a stronger 'kith and kin' attitude to every Israeli policy than the Conservative 'kith and kin' supporters of Ian Smith ever did. But stalinistic taboos on the left are stronger in Britain than on the right, and there is virtually no discussion even when the Labour Party supports Begin's government.

In the USA a similar situation prevails, and again the American liberals are the worst.

This is not the place to explore all the political consequences of this situation, but we must face reality: in our
struggle against the racism and fanaticism of the Jewish religion, our greatest enemies will be not only the Jewish racists
(and users of racism) but also those non-Jews who in other
areas are known – falsely in my opinion – as 'progressives'.

Chapter 3

Orthodoxy and Interpretation

This chapter is devoted to a more detailed description of the theologico-legal structure of classical Judaism.[1] However, before embarking on that description it is necessary to dispel at least some of the many misconceptions disseminated in almost all foreign-language (that is, non-Hebrew) accounts of Judaism, especially by those who propagate such currently fashionable phrases as 'the Judaeo-Christian tradition' or 'the common values of the monotheistic religions'.

Because of considerations of space I shall only deal in detail with the most important of these popular delusions: that the Jewish religion is, and always was, monotheistic. Now, as many biblical scholars know, and as a careful reading of the Old Testament easily reveals, this ahistorical view is quite wrong. In many, if not most, books of the Old Testament the existence and power of 'other gods' are clearly acknowledged, but Yahweh (Jehovah), who is the most powerful god,[2] is also very jealous of his rivals and forbids his people to worship them.[3] It is only very late in the Bible, in some of the later prophets, that the existence of all gods other than Yahweh is denied.[4]

What concerns us, however, is not biblical but classical Judaism; and it is quite clear, though much less widely realised, that the latter, during its last few hundred years, was for the most part far from pure monotheism. The same can be said about the real doctrines dominant in present-day Orthodox Judaism, which is a direct continuation of classical Judaism. The decay of monotheism came about through the spread of Jewish mysticism (the cabbala) which developed in the 12th and 13th centuries, and by the late 16th century had won an almost complete victory in virtually all the centres of Judaism. The Jewish Enlightenment, which arose out of the crisis of classical Judaism, had to fight against this mysticism and its influence more than against anything else, but in latter-day Jewish Orthodoxy, especially among the rabbis, the influence of the cabbala has remained predominant.[5] For example, the Gush Emunim movement is inspired to a great extent by cabbalistic ideas.

Knowledge and understanding of these ideas is therefore important for two reasons. First, without it one cannot understand the true beliefs of Judaism at the end of its classical period. Secondly, these ideas play an important contemporary political role, inasmuch as they form part of the explicit system of beliefs of many religious politicians, including most leaders of Gush Emunim, and have an indirect influence on many zionist leaders of all parties, including the zionist left.

According to the cabbala, the universe is ruled not by one god but by several deities, of various characters and influences, emanated by a dim, distant First Cause. Omitting many details, one can summarise the system as follows. From the First Cause, first a male god called 'Wisdom' or 'Father' and then a female goddess called 'Knowledge' or 'Mother' were emanated or born. From the marriage of these two, a pair of younger gods were born: Son, also called by many other names such as 'Small Face' or 'The Holy Blessed One'; and Daughter, also called 'Lady' (or 'Matronit', a word derived from Latin), 'Shekhinah', 'Queen', and so on. These two younger gods should be united, but their union is prevented by the machinations of Satan, who in this system is a very important and independent personage. The Creation was undertaken by the First Cause in order to allow them to unite, but because of the Fall they became more disunited than ever, and indeed Satan has managed to come very close to the divine Daughter and even to rape her (either seemingly or in fact – opinions differ on this). The creation of the Jewish people was undertaken in order to mend the break caused by Adam and Eve, and under Mount Sinai this was for a moment achieved: the male god Son, incarnated in Moses, was united with the goddess Shekhinah. Unfortunately, the sin of the Golden Calf again caused disunity in the godhead; but the repentance of the Jewish people has mended matters to some extent. Similarly, each incident of biblical Jewish history is believed to be associated with the union or disunion of the divine pair. The Jewish conquest of Palestine from the Canaanites and the building of the first and second Temple are particularly propitious for their union, while the destruction of the Temples and exile of the Jews from the Holy Land are merely external signs not only of the divine disunion but also of a real 'whoring after strange gods': Daughter falls closely into the power of Satan, while Son takes various female satanic personages to his bed, instead of his proper wife.

The duty of pious Jews is to restore through their prayers and religious acts the perfect divine unity, in the form of sexual union, between the male and female deities.[6] Thus before most ritual acts, which every devout Jew has to perform many times each day, the following cabbalistic formula is recited: 'For the sake of the [sexual] congress[7] of the Holy Blessed One and his Shekhinah ... ' The Jewish morning prayers are also arranged so as to promote this sexual union, if only temporarily. Successive parts of the prayer mystically correspond to successive stages of the union: at one point the goddess approaches with her handmaidens, at another the god puts his arm around her neck and fondles her breast, and finally the sexual act is supposed to take place.

Other prayers or religious acts, as interpreted by the cabbalists, are designed to deceive various angels (imagined as minor deities with a measure of independence) or to propitiate Satan. At a certain point in the morning prayer, some verses in Aramaic (rather than the more usual Hebrew) are pronounced.[8] This is supposed to be a means for tricking the angels who operate the gates through which prayers enter heaven and who have the power to block the prayers of the pious. The angels only understand Hebrew and are baffled by the Aramaic verses; being somewhat dull-witted (presumably they are far less clever than the cabbalists) they open the gates, and at this moment all the prayers, including those in Hebrew, get through. Or take another example: both before and after a meal, a pious Jew ritually washes his hands, uttering a special blessing. On one of these two occasions he is worshipping God, by promoting the divine union of Son and Daughter; but on the other he is worshipping Satan, who likes Jewish prayers and ritual acts so much that when he is offered a few of them it keeps him busy for a while and he forgets to pester the divine Daughter. Indeed, the cabbalists believe that some of the sacrifices burnt in the Temple were intended for Satan. For example, the seventy bullocks sacrificed during the seven days of the feast of Tabernacles,[9] were supposedly offered to Satan in his capacity as ruler of all the Gentiles,[10] in order to keep him too busy to interfere on the eighth day, when sacrifice is made to God. Many other examples of the same kind can be given.

Several points should be made concerning this system and its importance for the proper understanding of Judaism, both in its classical period and in its present political involvement in zionist practice.

First, whatever can be said about this cabbalistic system, it cannot be regarded as monotheistic, unless one is also prepared to regard Hinduism, the late Graeco-Roman religion, or even the religion of ancient Egypt, as 'monotheistic'.

Secondly, the real nature of classical Judaism is illustrated by the ease with which this system was adopted. Faith and beliefs (except nationalistic beliefs) play an extremely small part in classical Judaism. What is of prime importance is the ritual act, rather than the significance which that act is supposed to have or the belief attached to it. Therefore in times when a minority of religious Jews refused to accept the cabbala (as is the case today), one could see some few Jews performing a given religious ritual believing it to be an act of worship of God, while others do exactly the same thing with the intention of propitiating Satan – but so long as the act is the same they would pray together and remain members of the same congregation, however much they might dislike each other. But if instead of the *intention* attached to the ritual washing of hands anyone would dare to introduce an innovation in the *manner* of washing,[11] a real schism would certainly ensue.

The same can be said about all sacred formulas of Judaism. Provided the wording is left intact, the meaning is at best a secondary matter. For example, perhaps the most sacred Jewish formula, 'Hear O Israel, the Lord is our God, the Lord is one', recited several times each day by every pious Jew, can at the present time mean two contrary things. It can mean that the Lord is indeed 'one'; but it can also mean that a certain stage in the union of the male and female deities has been reached or is being promoted by the proper recitation of this formula. However, when Jews of a Reformed congregation recite this formula in any language other than Hebrew, all Orthodox rabbis, whether they believe in unity or in the divine sexual union, are very angry indeed.

Finally, all this is of considerable importance in Israel (and in other Jewish centres) even at present. The enormous significance attached to mere formulas (such as the 'Law of Jerusalem'); the ideas and motivations of Gush Emunim; the urgency behind the hate for non-Jews presently living in Palestine; the fatalistic attitude towards all peace attempts by Arab states – all these and many other traits of zionist politics, which puzzle so many well-meaning people who have a false notion about classical Judaism, become more intelligible against this religious and mystical background. I must warn, however, against falling into the other extreme and trying to explain all zionist politics in terms of this background. Obviously, the latter's influences vary in extent. Ben-Gurion was adept at manipulating them in a controlled way for specific ends. Under Begin the past exerted a much greater influence upon the present. But what one should never do is to ignore the past and its influences, because only by knowing it can one transcend its blind power.

Interpretation of the Bible

It will be seen from the foregoing example that what most supposedly well-informed people think they know about Judaism may be very misleading, unless they can read Hebrew. All the details mentioned above can be found in the original texts or, in some cases, in modern books written in Hebrew for a rather specialised readership. In English one would look for them in vain, even where the omission of such socially important facts distorts the whole picture.

There is yet another misconception about Judaism which is particularly common among Christians, or people heavily influ-enced by Christian tradition and culture. This is the misleading idea that Judaism is a 'biblical religion'; that the Old Testament has in Judaism the same central place and legal authority which the Bible has for Protestant or even Catholic Christianity.

Again, this is connected with the question of interpretation. We have seen that in matters of belief there is great latitude. Exactly the opposite holds with respect to the legal interpreta-tion of sacred texts. Here the interpretation is rigidly fixed – but by the Talmud rather than by the Bible itself.[12] Many, perhaps most, biblical verses prescribing religious acts and obli-gations are 'understood' by classical Judaism, and by present-day Orthodoxy, in a sense which is quite distinct from, or even contrary to, their literal meaning as understood by Christian or other readers of the Old Testament, who only see the plain text. The same division exists at present in Israel between those educated in Jewish religious schools and those educated in 'secular' Hebrew schools, where on the whole the plain meaning of the Old Testament is taught.

This important point can only be understood through exam-ples. It will be noted that the changes in meaning do not all go in the same direction from the point of view of ethics, as the term is understood now. Apologetics of Judaism claim that the interpretation of the Bible, originated by the Pharisees and fixed in the Talmud, is always more liberal than the literal sense. But some of the examples below show that this is far from being the case.

1 Let us start with the Decalogue itself. The Eighth Command-ment, 'Thou shalt not steal' (*Exodus*, 20:15), is taken to be a prohibition against 'stealing' (that is, kidnapping) *a Jewish person*. The reason is that according to the Talmud all acts forbidden by the Decalogue are capital offences. Stealing property is not a capital offence (while kidnapping of Gentiles by Jews is allowed by talmudic law) – hence the interpretation. A virtually identical

sentence – 'Ye shall not steal' (*Leviticus*, 19:11) – is however allowed to have its literal meaning.

2 The famous verse 'Eye for eye, tooth for tooth' etc. (*Exodus*, 21:24) is taken to mean 'eye-money for eye', that is payment of a fine rather than physical retribution.

3 Here is a notorious case of turning the literal meaning into its exact opposite. The biblical text plainly warns against following the bandwagon in an unjust cause: 'Thou shalt not follow a multitude to do evil; neither shalt thou speak in a cause to decline after many to wrest judgement' (*Exodus*, 23:2). The last words of this sentence – 'Decline after many to wrest judgement' – are torn out of their context and interpreted as an injunction to follow the majority!

4 The verse 'Thou shalt not seethe a kid in his mother's milk' (*Exodus*, 23:19) is interpreted as a ban on mixing any kind of meat with any milk or milk product. Since the same verse is repeated in two other places in the Pentateuch, the mere repetition is taken to be a treble ban, forbidding a Jew (i) to eat such a mixture, (ii) to cook it for any purpose and (iii) to enjoy or benefit from it in any way.[13]

5 In numerous cases general terms such as 'thy fellow', 'stranger', or even 'man' are taken to have an exclusivist chauvinistic meaning. The famous verse 'thou shalt love thy fellow[14] as thyself' (*Leviticus*, 19:18) is understood by classical (and present-day Orthodox) Judaism as an injunction to love one's fellow Jew, not any fellow human. Similarly, the verse 'neither shalt thou stand against the blood of thy fellow' (*ibid.*, 16) is supposed to mean that one must not stand idly by when the life ('blood') of a fellow *Jew* is in danger; but, as will be seen in Chapter 5, a Jew is in general forbidden to save the life of a Gentile, because 'he is not thy fellow'. The generous injunction to leave the gleanings of one's field and vineyard 'for the poor and the stranger' (*ibid.*, 9–10) is interpreted as referring exclusively to the *Jewish* poor and to converts to Judaism. The taboo laws relating to corpses begin with the verse 'This is the law, when a man dieth in a tent: all that come into the tent ... shall be unclean seven days' (*Numbers*, 19:14). But the word 'man' (*adam*) is taken to mean 'Jew', so that only a Jewish corpse is taboo (that is, both 'unclean' and sacred). Based on this interpretation, pious Jews have a tremendous magic reverence towards Jewish corpses and Jewish cemeteries, but have no respect towards non-Jewish corpses and cemeteries. Thus hundreds of Muslim cemeteries have been utterly destroyed in Israel (in one case in order to make room

for the Tel-Aviv Hilton) but there was a great outcry because the Jewish cemetery on the Mount of Olives was damaged under Jordanian rule. Examples of this kind are too numerous to quote. Some of the inhuman consequences of this type of interpretation will be discussed in Chapter 5.

6 Finally, consider one of the most beautiful prophetic passages, Isaiah's magnificent condemnation of hypocrisy and empty ritual, and exhortation to common decency. One verse (*Isaiah*, 1:15) in this passage is: 'And when ye spread forth your hands, I will hide mine eyes from you; yea, when ye make many prayers, I will not hear: your hands are full of blood.' Since Jewish priests 'spread their hands' when blessing the people during service, this verse is supposed to mean that a priest who commits accidental homicide is disqualified from 'spreading his hands' in blessing (even if repentant) because they are 'full of blood'.

It is quite clear even from these examples that when Orthodox Jews today (or all Jews before about 1780) read the Bible, they are reading a very different book, with a totally different meaning, from the Bible as read by non-Jews or non-Orthodox Jews. This distinction applies even in Israel, although both parties read the text in Hebrew. Experience, particularly since 1967, has repeatedly corroborated this. Many Jews in Israel (and elsewhere), who are not Orthodox and have little detailed knowledge of the Jewish religion, have tried to shame Orthodox Israelis (or right-wingers who are strongly influenced by religion) out of their inhuman attitude towards the Palestinians, by quoting at them verses from the Bible in their plain humane sense. It was always found, however, that such arguments do not have the slightest effect on those who follow classical Judaism; they simply do not understand what is being said to them, because to them the biblical text means something quite different than to everyone else.

If such a communication gap exists in Israel, where people read Hebrew and can readily obtain correct information if they wish, one can imagine how deep is the misconception abroad, say among people educated in the Christian tradition. In fact, the more such a person reads the Bible, the less he or she knows about Orthodox Judaism. For the latter regards the Old Testament as a text of immutable sacred formulas, whose recitation is an act of great merit, but whose meaning is wholly determined elsewhere. And, as Humpty Dumpty told Alice, behind the problem of who can determine the meaning of words, there stands the real question: 'Which is to be master?'

Structure of the Talmud

It should therefore be clearly understood that the source of authority for all the practices of classical (and present-day Orthodox) Judaism, the determining base of its legal structure, is the Talmud, or, to be precise, the so-called Babylonian Talmud; while the rest of the talmudic literature (including the so-called Jerusalem or Palestinian Talmud) acts as a supplementary authority.

We cannot enter here into a detailed description of the Talmud and talmudic literature, but confine ourselves to a few principal points needed for our argument. Basically, the Talmud consists of two parts. First, the Mishnah – a terse legal code consisting of six volumes, each subdivided into several *tractates*, written in Hebrew, redacted in Palestine around AD 200 out of the much more extensive (and largely oral) legal material composed during the preceding two centuries. The second and by far predominant part is the Gemarah – a voluminous record of discussions on and around the Mishnah. There are two, roughly parallel, sets of Gemarah, one composed in Mesopotamia ('Babylon') between about AD 200 and 500, the other in Palestine between about AD 200 and some unknown date long before 500. The Babylonian Talmud (that is, the Mishnah plus the Mesopotamian Gemarah) is much more extensive and better arranged than the Palestinian, and it alone is regarded as definitive and authoritative. The Jerusalem (Palestinian) Talmud is accorded a decidedly lower status as a legal authority, along with a number of compilations, known collectively as the 'talmudic literature', containing material which the editors of the two Talmuds had left out.

Contrary to the Mishnah, the rest of the Talmud and talmudic literature is written in a mixture of Hebrew and Aramaic, the latter language predominating in the Babylonian Talmud. Also, it is not limited to legal matters. Without any apparent order or reason, the legal discussion can suddenly be interrupted by what is referred to as 'Narrative' (*Aggadah*) – a medley of tales and anecdotes about rabbis or ordinary folk, biblical figures, angels, demons, witchcraft and miracles.[15] These narrative passages, although of great popular influence in Judaism through the ages, were always considered (even by the Talmud itself) as having secondary value. Of greatest importance for classical Judaism are the legal parts of the text, particularly the discussion of cases which are regarded as problematic. The Talmud itself defines the various categories of Jews, in ascending order, as follows. The lowest are the totally ignorant, then come those who only know the Bible, then those who are familiar with the Mishnah or

Aggadah, and the superior class are those who have studied, and are able to discuss the legal part of the Gemarah. It is only the latter who are fit to lead their fellow Jews in all things.

The legal system of the Talmud can be described as totally comprehensive, rigidly authoritarian, and yet capable of infinite development, without however any change in its dogmatic base. Every aspect of Jewish life, both individual and social, is covered, usually in considerable detail, with sanctions and punishments provided for every conceivable sin or infringement of the rules. The basic rules for every problem are stated dogmatically and cannot be questioned. What can be and is discussed at very great length is the elaboration and practical definition of these rules. Let me give a few examples.

'Not doing any work' on the sabbath. The concept *work* is defined as comprising exactly 39 types of work, neither more nor less. The criterion for inclusion in this list has nothing to do with the arduousness of a given task; it is simply a matter of dogmatic definition. One forbidden type of 'work' is writing. The question then arises: How many characters must one write in order to commit the sin of writing on the sabbath? (Answer: Two). Is the sin the same, irrespective of which hand is used? (Answer: No). However, in order to guard against falling into sin, the primary prohibition on writing is hedged with a secondary ban on touching any writing implement on the sabbath.

Another prototypical work forbidden on the sabbath is the grinding of grain. From this it is deduced, by analogy, that any kind of grinding of anything whatsoever is forbidden. And this in turn is hedged by a ban on the practice of medicine on the sabbath (except in cases of danger to Jewish life), in order to guard against falling into the sin of grinding a medicament. It is in vain to point out that in modern times such a danger does not exist (nor, for that matter, did it exist in many cases even in talmudic times); for, as a hedge around the hedge, the Talmud explicitly forbids liquid medicines and restorative drinks on the sabbath. What has been fixed remains for ever fixed, however absurd. Tertullian, one of the early Church Fathers, had written, 'I believe it because it is absurd.' This can serve as a motto for the majority of talmudic rules, with the word 'believe' replaced by 'practise'.

The following example illustrates even better the level of absurdity reached by this system. One of the prototypes of work forbidden on the sabbath is harvesting. This is stretched, by analogy, to a ban on breaking a branch off a tree. Hence, riding a horse (or any other animal) is forbidden, as a hedge against the temptation to break a branch off a tree for flogging the beast. It is useless to argue that you have a ready-made whip, or that you intend to ride where there are no trees. What is forbidden remains forbidden for ever. It can, however, be stretched and made stricter: in modern times, riding a bicycle on the sabbath has been forbidden, because it is analogous to riding a horse.

My final example illustrates how the same methods are used also in purely theoretical cases, having no conceivable application in reality. During the existence of the Temple, the High Priest was only allowed to marry a virgin. Although during virtually the whole of the talmudic period there was no longer a Temple or a High Priest, the Talmud devotes one of its more involved (and bizarre) discussions to the precise definition of the term 'virgin' fit to marry a High Priest. What about a woman whose hymen had been broken by accident? Does it make any difference whether the accident occurred before or after the age of three? By the impact of metal or of wood? Was she climbing a tree? And if so, was she climbing up or down? Did it happen naturally or unnaturally? All this and much else besides is discussed in lengthy detail. And every scholar in classical Judaism had to master hundreds of such problems. Great scholars were measured by their ability to develop these problems still further, for as shown by the examples there is always scope for further development – if only in one direction – and such development did actually continue after the final redaction of the Talmud.

However, there are two great differences between the talmudic period (ending around AD 500) and the period of classical Judaism (from about AD 800). The geographical area reflected in the Talmud is confined, whereas the Jewish society reflected in it is a 'complete' society, with Jewish agriculture as its basis. (This is true for Mesopotamia as well as Palestine.) Although at that time there were Jews living throughout the Roman Empire and in many areas of the Sassanid Empire, it is quite evident from the talmudic text that its composition – over half a millennium – was a strictly local affair. No scholars from countries other than Mesopotamia and Palestine took part in it, nor does the text reflect social conditions outside these two areas.

Very little is known about the social and religious conditions of the Jews in the intervening three centuries. But from AD 800 on, when more detailed historical information is again available, we find that the two features mentioned above had been reversed. The Babylonian Talmud (and to a much lesser degree the rest of the talmudic literature) is acknowledged as authoritative, studied and developed in all Jewish communities. At the same time, Jewish society had undergone a deep change: whatever and wherever it is, *it does not include peasants.*

The social system resulting from this change will be discussed in Chapter 4. Here we shall describe how the Talmud was adapted to the conditions – geographically much wider and socially much narrower, and at any rate radically different – of classical Judaism. We shall concentrate on what is in my opinion the most important method of adaptation, namely the dispensations.

The Dispensations

As noted above, the talmudic system is most dogmatic and does not allow any relaxation of its rules even when they are reduced to absurdity by a change in circumstances. And in the case of the Talmud – contrary to that of the Bible – the *literal* sense of the text is binding, and one is not allowed to interpret it away. But in the period of classical Judaism various talmudic laws became untenable for the Jewish ruling classes – the rabbis and the rich. In the interest of these ruling classes, a method of systematic deception was devised for keeping the letter of the law, while violating its spirit and intention. It was this hypocritical system of 'dispensations' (*heterim*) which, in my view, was the most important cause of the debasement of Judaism in its classical epoch. (The second cause was Jewish mysticism, which however operated for a much shorter period of time.) Again, some examples are needed to illustrate how the system works.

1 *Taking of interest.* The Talmud strictly forbids a Jew, on pain of severe punishment, to take interest on a loan made to another Jew. (According to a majority of talmudic authorities, it is a religious duty to take as much interest as possible on a loan made to a Gentile.) Very detailed rules forbid even the most far-fetched forms in which a Jewish lender might benefit from a Jewish debtor. All Jewish accomplices to such an illicit transaction, including the scribe and the witnesses, are branded by the Talmud as infamous persons, disqualified from testifying in court, because by participating in such an act a Jew as good as declares that 'he has no part in the god of Israel'. It is evident that this law is well suited to the needs of Jewish peasants or artisans, or of small Jewish communities who use their money for lending to non-Jews. But the situation was very different in east Europe (mainly in Poland) by the 16th century. There was a relatively big Jewish community, which

constituted the majority in many towns. The peasants, subjected to strict serfdom not far removed from slavery, were hardly in a position to borrow at all, while lending to the nobility was the business of a few very rich Jews. Many Jews were doing business with each other.

In these circumstances, the following arrangement (called *heter 'isqa* – 'business dispensation') was devised for an interest-bearing loan between Jews, which does not violate the letter of the law, because formally it is not a loan at all. The lender 'invests' his money in the business of the borrower, stipulating two conditions. First, that the borrower will pay the lender at an agreed future date a stated sum of money (in reality, the interest in the loan) as the lender's 'share in the profits'. Secondly, that the borrower will be presumed to have made sufficient profit to give the lender his share, unless a claim to the contrary is corroborated by the testimony of the town's rabbi or rabbinical judge, etc. – who, by arrangement, refuse to testify in such cases. In practice all that is required is to take a text of this dispensation, written in Aramaic and entirely incomprehensible to the great majority, and put it on a wall of the room where the transaction is made (a copy of this text is displayed in all branches of Israeli banks) or even to keep it in a chest – and the interest-bearing loan between Jews becomes perfectly legal and blameless.

2 *The sabbatical year*. According to talmudic law (based on *Leviticus*, 25) Jewish-owned land in Palestine[16] must be left fallow every seventh ('sabbatical') year, when all agricultural work (including harvesting) on such land is forbidden. There is ample evidence that this law was rigorously observed for about one thousand years, from the 5th century BC till the disappearance of Jewish agriculture in Palestine. Later, when there was no occasion to apply the law in practice, it was kept theoretically intact. However, in the 1880s, with the establishment of the first Jewish agricultural colonies in Palestine, it became a matter of practical concern. Rabbis sympathetic to the settlers helpfully devised a dispensation, which was later perfected by their successors in the religious zionist parties and has become an established Israeli practice.

This is how it works. Shortly before a sabbatical year, the Israeli Minister of Internal Affairs gives the Chief Rabbi a document making him the legal owner of all Israeli land, both private and public. Armed with this paper, the Chief Rabbi goes to a non-Jew and sells him all the land of Israel (and, since 1967, the Occupied Territories) for a nominal sum. A separate document stipulates that the 'buyer' will 'resell' the

land back after the year is over. And this transaction is repeated every seven years, usually with the same 'buyer'.

Non-zionist rabbis do not recognise the validity of this
dispensation,[17] claiming correctly that, since religious law forbids Jews to sell land in Palestine to Gentiles, the whole
transaction is based on a sin and hence null and void. The
zionist rabbis reply, however, that what is forbidden is a real
sale, not a fictitious one!

3 *Milking on the sabbath.* This has been forbidden in post-
talmudic times, through the process of increasing religious
severity mentioned above. The ban could easily be kept in the
diaspora, since Jews who had cows of their own were usually
rich enough to have non-Jewish servants, who could be ordered
(using one of the subterfuges described below) to do the
milking. The early Jewish colonists in Palestine employed Arabs
for this and other purposes, but with the forcible imposition of
the zionist policy of exclusive Jewish labour there was need for
a dispensation. (This was particularly important before the
introduction of mechanised milking in the late 1950s.) Here
too there was a difference between zionist and non-zionist
rabbis.

According to the former, the forbidden milking becomes
permitted provided the milk is not white but dyed blue. This
blue Saturday milk is then used exclusively for making cheese,
and the dye is washed off into the whey. Non-zionist rabbis
have devised a much subtler scheme (which I personally witnessed operating in a religious kibbutz in 1952). They discovered an old provision which allows the udders of a cow to be
emptied on the sabbath, purely for relieving the suffering
caused to the animal by bloated udders, and on the strict
condition that the milk runs to waste on the ground. Now, this
is what is actually done: on Saturday morning, a pious kibbut-
znik goes to the cowshed and places pails under the cows.
(There is no ban on such work in the whole of the talmudic
literature.) He then goes to the synagogue to pray. Then comes
his colleague, whose 'honest intention' is to relieve the animals'
pain and let their milk run to the floor. But if, by chance, a
pail happens to be standing there, is he under any obligation to
remove it? Of course not. He simply 'ignores' the pails, fulfills
his mission of mercy and goes to the synagogue. Finally a third
pious colleague goes into the cowshed and discovers, to his
great surprise, the pails full of milk. So he puts them in cold
storage and follows his comrades to the synagogue. Now all is
well, and there is no need to waste money on blue dye.

4 *Mixed crops.* Similar dispensations were issued by zionist rabbis

in respect of the ban (based on *Leviticus*, 19:19) against sowing two different species of crop in the same field. Modern agronomy has however shown that in some cases (especially in growing fodder) mixed sowing is the most profitable. The rabbis invented a dispensation according to which one man sows the field length-wise with one kind of seed, and later that day his comrade, who 'does not know' about the former, sows another kind of seed crosswise. However, this method was felt to be too wasteful of labour, and a better one was devised: one man makes a heap of one kind of seed in a public place and carefully covers it with a sack or piece of board. The second kind of seed is then put on top of the cover. Later, another man comes and exclaims, in front of witnesses, 'I need this sack (or board)' and removes it, so that the seeds mix 'naturally'. Finally, a third man comes along and is told,'Take this and sow the field,' which he proceeds to do.[18]

5 *Leavened substances* must not be eaten or even kept in the possession of a Jew during the seven (or, outside Palestine, eight) days of Passover. The concept 'leavened substances' was continually broadened and the aversion to so much as seeing them during the festival approached hysteria. They include all kinds of flour and even unground grain. In the original talmudic society this was bearable, because bread (leavened or not) was usually baked once a week; a peasant family would use the last of the previous year's grain to bake unleavened bread for the festival, which ushers in the new harvest season. However, in the conditions of post-Talmudic European Jewry the observance was very hard on a middle-class Jewish family and even more so on a corn merchant. A dispensation was therefore devised, by which all those substances are sold in a fictitious sale to a Gentile before the festival and bought back automatically after it. The one thing that must be done is to lock up the taboo substances for the duration of the festival. In Israel this fictitious sale has been made more efficient. Religious Jews 'sell' their leavened substances to their local rabbis, who in turn 'sell' them to the Chief Rabbis; the latter sell them to a Gentile, and by a special dispensation this sale is presumed to include also the leavened substances of non-practising Jews.

6 *Sabbath-Goy*. Perhaps the most developed dispensations concern the 'Goy (Gentile) of Sabbath'. As mentioned above, the range of tasks banned on the sabbath has widened continually; but the range of tasks that must be carried out or supervised to satisfy needs or to increase comfort also keeps widening. This is particularly true in modern times, but the effect of technological change began to be felt long ago. The ban against grinding on the

sabbath was a relatively light matter for a Jewish peasant or artisan, say in second-century Palestine, who used a hand mill for domestic purposes. It was quite a different matter for a tenant of a water mill or windmill – one of the most common Jewish occupations in eastern Europe. But even such a simple human 'problem' as the wish to have a hot cup of tea on a Saturday afternoon becomes much greater with the tempting samovar, used regularly on weekdays, standing in the room. These are just two examples out of a very large number of so-called 'problems of sabbath observance'. And one can state with certainty that for a community composed exclusively of Orthodox Jews they were quite insoluble, at least during the last eight or ten centuries, without the 'help' of non-Jews. This is even more true today in the 'Jewish state', because many public services, such as water, gas and electricity, fall in this category. Classical Judaism could not exist even for a whole week without using some non-Jews.

But without special dispensations there is a great obstacle in employing non-Jews to do these Saturday jobs; for talmudic regulations forbid Jews to ask a Gentile to do on the sabbath any work which they themselves are banned from doing.[19] I shall describe two of the many types of dispensation used for such purposes.

First, there is the method of 'hinting', which depends on the casuistic logic according to which a sinful demand becomes blameless if it is phrased slyly. As rule, the hint must be 'obscure', but in cases of extreme need a 'clear' hint is allowed. For example, in a recent booklet on religious observance for the use of Israeli soldiers, the latter are taught how to talk to Arab workers employed by the army as sabbath-Goyim. In urgent cases, such as when it is very cold and a fire must be lit, or when light is needed for a religious service, a pious Jewish soldier may use a 'clear' hint and tell the Arab: 'It is cold (or dark) here'. But normally an 'obscure' hint must suffice, for example: 'It would be more pleasant if it were warmer here.'[20] This method of 'hinting' is particularly repulsive and degrading inasmuch as it is normally used on non-Jews who, due to their poverty or subordinate social position, are wholly in the power of their Jewish employer. A Gentile servant (or employee of the Israeli army) who does not train himself to interpret 'obscure hints' as orders will be pitilessly dismissed.

The second method is used in cases where what the Gentile is required to do on Saturday is not an occasional task or personal service, which can be 'hinted' at as the need arises, but a routine or regular job without constant Jewish supervision. According to this method – called 'implicit inclusion' (havla'ah) of the sabbath among weekdays – the Gentile is hired 'for the whole week (or year)', without the sabbath being so much as mentioned in the contract. But in reality work is only performed on the sabbath. This method was used in the past in hiring a Gentile to put out the candles in the synagogue after the sabbath-eve prayer (rather than wastefully allowing them to burn out). Modern Israeli examples are: regulating the water supply or watching over water reservoirs on Saturdays.[21]

A similar idea is used also in the case of Jews, but for a different end. Jews are forbidden to receive any payment for work done on the sabbath, even if the work itself is permitted. The chief example here concerns the sacred professions: the rabbi or talmudic scholar who preaches or teaches on the sabbath, the cantor who sings only on Saturdays and other holy days (on which similar bans apply), the sexton and similar officials. In talmudic times, and in some countries even several centuries after, such jobs were unpaid. But later, when these became salaried professions, the dispensation of 'implicit inclusion' was used, and they were hired on a 'monthly' or 'yearly' basis. In the case of rabbis and talmudic scholars the problem is particularly complicated, because the Talmud forbids them to receive any payment for preaching, teaching or studying talmudic matters even on weekdays.[22] For them an additional dispensation stipulates that their salary is not really a salary at all but 'compensation for idleness' (dmey batalah). As a combined result of these two fictions, what is in reality payment for *work* done mainly, or even solely, on the *sabbath* is transmogrified into payment for being *idle* on *weekdays*.

Social Aspects of Dispensations

Two social features of these and many similar practices deserve special mention.

First, a dominant feature of this system of dispensations, and of classical Judaism inasmuch as it is based on them, is deception – deception primarily of God, if this word can be used for an imaginary being so easily deceived by the rabbis, who consider themselves cleverer than him. No greater contrast can be conceived than that between the God of the Bible (particularly of the greater prophets) and of the God of classical Judaism. The latter is more like the early Roman Jupiter, who was likewise bamboozled by his worshippers, or the gods described in Frazer's *Golden Bough*.

From the ethical point of view, classical Judaism represents a process of degeneration, which is still going on; and this degeneration into a tribal collection of empty rituals and magic superstitions has very important social and political consequences. For it must be remembered that it is precisely the superstitions of classical Judaism which have the greatest hold on the Jewish masses, rather than those parts of the Bible or even the Talmud which are of real religious and ethical value. (The same can be observed also in other religions which are now undergoing revival.) What is popularly regarded as the most 'holy' and solemn occasion of the Jewish liturgical year, attended even by very many Jews who are otherwise far from religion? It is the *Kol Nidrey* prayer on the eve of Yom Kippur – a chanting of a particularly absurd and deceptive dispensation, by which all private vows made to God in the following year are declared in advance to be null and void.[23] Or, in the area of personal religion, the *Qadish* prayer, said on days of mourning by sons for their parents in order to elevate their departed souls to paradise – a recitation of an Aramaic text, incomprehensible to the great majority. Quite obviously, the popular regard given to these, the most superstitious parts of the Jewish religion, is not given to its better parts.

Together with the deception of God goes the deception of other Jews, mainly in the interest of the Jewish ruling class. It is characteristic that no dispensations were allowed in the specific interest of the Jewish poor. For example, Jews who were starving but not actually on the point of death were never allowed by their rabbis (who did not often go hungry themselves) to eat any sort of forbidden food, though kosher food is usually more expensive.

The second dominant feature of the dispensations is that they are in large part obviously motivated by the spirit of profit. And it is this combination of hypocrisy and the profit motive which increasingly dominated classical Judaism. In Israel, where the process goes on, this is dimly perceived by popular opinion, despite all the official brainwashing promoted by the education system and the media. The religious establishment – the rabbis and the religious parties – and, by association, to some extent the Orthodox community as a whole, are quite unpopular in Israel. One of the most important reasons for this is precisely their reputation for duplicity and venality. Of course, popular opinion (which may often be prejudiced) is not the same thing as social analysis; but in this particular case it is actually true that the Jewish religious establishment does have a strong tendency to chicanery and graft, due to the corrupting influence of the Orthodox Jewish religion. Because in general social life religion is only one of the social influences, its effect on the mass of believers is

not nearly so great as on the rabbis and leaders of the
religious parties. Those religious Jews in Israel who are honest, as the majority of them undoubtedly are, are so not
because of the influence of their religion and rabbis, but in
spite of it. On the other hand, in those few areas of public
life in Israel which are wholly dominated by religious circles,
the level of chicanery, venality and corruption is notorious,
far surpassing the 'average' level tolerated by general, non-
religious Israeli society.

In Chapter 4 we shall see how the dominance of the profit
motive in classical Judaism is connected with the structure of
Jewish society and its articulation with the general society in
the midst of which Jews lived in the 'classical' period. Here I
merely want to observe that the profit motive is not characteristic of Judaism in all periods of its history. Only the platonist
confusion which seeks for the metaphysical timeless 'essence' of
Judaism, instead of looking at the historical changes in Jewish
society, has obscured this fact. (And this confusion has been
greatly encouraged by zionism, in its reliance on 'historical
rights' ahistorically derived from the Bible.) Thus, apologists of
Judaism claim, quite correctly, that the Bible is hostile to the
profit motive while the Talmud is indifferent to it. But this was
caused by the very different social conditions in which they
were composed. As was pointed out above, the Talmud was
composed in two well-defined areas, in a period when the Jews
living there constituted a society based on agriculture and
consisting mainly of peasants – very different indeed from the
society of classical Judaism.

In Chapter 5 we shall deal in detail with the hostile attitudes and deceptions practised by classical Judaism against
non-Jews. But more important as a social feature is the profit-
motivated deception practised by the rich Jews against poor
fellow Jews (such as the dispensation concerning interest on
loans). Here I must say, in spite of my opposition to marxism
both in philosophy and as a social theory, that Marx was quite
right when, in his two articles about Judaism, he characterised
it as dominated by profit-seeking – provided this is limited to
Judaism as he knew it, that is, to classical Judaism which in his
youth had already entered the period of its dissolution. True,
he stated this arbitrarily, ahistorically and without proof. Obviously he came to his conclusion by intuition; but his intuition
in this case – and with the proper historical limitation – was
right.

Chapter 4

The Weight of History

A great deal of nonsense has been written in the attempt to provide a social or mystical interpretation of Jewry or Judaism 'as a whole'. This cannot be done, for the social structure of the Jewish people and the ideological structure of Judaism have changed profoundly through the ages. Four major phases can be distinguished:

1 The phase of the ancient kingdoms of Israel and Judah, until the destruction the first Temple (587 BC) and the Babylonian exile. (Much of the Old Testament is concerned with this period, although most major books of the Old Testament, including the Pentateuch as we know it, were actually composed after that date.) Socially, these ancient Jewish kingdoms were quite similar to the neighbouring kingdoms of Palestine and Syria; and – as a careful reading of the Prophets reveals – the similarity extended to the religious cults practised by the great majority of the people.[1] The ideas that were to become typical of later Judaism – including in particular ethnic segregationism and monotheistic exclusivism – were at this stage confined to small circles of priests and prophets, whose social influence depended on royal support.

2 The phase of the dual centres, Palestine and Mesopotamia, from the first 'Return from Babylon' (537 BC) until about AD 500. It is characterised by the existence of these two autonomous Jewish societies, both based primarily on agriculture, on which the 'Jewish religion', as previously elaborated in priestly and scribal circles, was imposed by the force and authority of the Persian empire. The Old Testament Book of Ezra contains an account of the activities of Ezra the priest, 'a ready scribe in the law of Moses', who was empowered by King Artaxerxes I of Persia to 'set magistrates and judges' over the Jews of Palestine, so that 'whosoever will not do the law of thy God, and the law of the king, let judgement be executed speedily upon him, whether it be unto death, or to banishment, or to confiscation of goods, or to imprisonment.'[2] And in the Book of Nehemiah – cupbearer to King Artaxerxes who was appointed Persian governor of Judea, with even greater powers – we see to what extent foreign (nowadays one would say 'imperialist') coercion was instrumental in imposing the Jewish religion, *with lasting results*.

In both centres, Jewish autonomy persisted during most of this period and deviations from religious orthodoxy were repressed. Exceptions to this rule occurred when the religious aristocracy itself got 'infected' with Hellenistic ideas (from 300 to 166 BC and again under Herod the Great and his successors, from 50 BC to AD 70), or when it was split in reaction to new developments (for example, the division between the two great parties, the Pharisees and the Sadduceans, which emerged in about 140 BC). However, the moment any one party triumphed, it used the coercive machinery of the Jewish autonomy (or, for a short period, independence) to impose its own religious views on all the Jews in both centres.

During most of this time, especially after the collapse of the Persian empire and until about AD 200, the Jews outside the two centres were free from Jewish religious coercion. Among the papyri preserved in Elephantine (in Upper Egypt) there is a letter dating from 419 BC containing the text of an edict by King Darius II of Persia which instructs the Jews of Egypt as to the details of the observance of Passover.[3] But the Hellenistic kingdoms, the Roman Republic and early Roman Empire did not bother with such things. The freedom that Hellenistic Jews enjoyed outside Palestine allowed the creation of a Jewish literature written in Greek, which was subsequently rejected *in toto* by Judaism and whose remains were preserved by Christianity.[4] The very rise of Christianity was possible because of this relative freedom of the Jewish communities *outside* the two centres. The experience of the Apostle Paul is significant: in Corinth, when the local Jewish community accused Paul of heresy, the Roman governor Gallio dismissed the case at once, refusing to be a 'judge of such matters';[5] but in Judea the governor Festus felt *obliged* to take legal cognizance of a purely religious internal Jewish dispute.[6]

This tolerance came to an end in about AD 200, when the Jewish religion, as meanwhile elaborated and evolved in Palestine, was imposed by the Roman authorities upon all the Jews of the Empire.[7]

3 The phase which we have defined as *classical Judaism* and which will be discussed below.[8]

4 The modern phase, characterised by the breakdown of the totalitarian Jewish community and its power, and by attempts to reimpose it, of which zionism is the most important. This phase begins in Holland in the 17th century, in France and Austria (excluding Hungary) in the late 18th century, in most other European countries in the middle of the 19th century, and in

some Islamic countries in the 20th century. (The Jews of Yemen were still living in the medieval 'classical' phase in 1948). Something concerning these developments will be said later on.

Between the second phase and the third, that of classical Judaism, there is a gap of several centuries in which our present knowledge of Jews and Jewish society is very slight, and the scant information we do have is all derived from external (non-Jewish) sources. In the countries of Latin Christendom we have absolutely no Jewish literary records until the middle of the 10th century; internal Jewish information, mostly from religious literature, becomes more abundant only in the 11th and particularly the 12th century. Before that, we are wholly dependent first on Roman and then on Christian evidence. In the Islamic countries the information gap is not quite so big; still, very little is known about Jewish society before AD 800 and about the changes it must have undergone during the three preceding centuries.

Major Features of Classical Judaism

Let us therefore ignore those 'dark ages', and for the sake of convenience begin with the two centuries 1000–1200, for which abundant information is available from both internal and external sources on all the important Jewish centres, east and west. Classical Judaism, which is clearly discernible in this period, has undergone very few changes since then, and (in the guise of Orthodox Judaism) is still a powerful force today.

How can that classical Judaism be characterised, and what are the *social* differences distinguishing it from earlier phases of Judaism? I believe that there are three such major features.

1 *Classical Jewish society has no peasants*, and in this it differs profoundly from earlier Jewish societies in the two centres, Palestine and Mesopotamia. It is difficult for us, in modern times, to understand what this means. We have to make an effort to imagine what serfdom was like; the enormous difference in literacy, let alone education, between village and town throughout this period; the incomparably greater freedom enjoyed by *all* the small minority who were not peasants – in order to realise that during the whole of the classical period the Jews, in spite of all the persecutions to which they were subjected, formed an integral part of the privileged classes. Jewish historiography, especially in English, is misleading on this point inasmuch as it tends to focus on Jewish poverty and anti-Jewish discrimination. Both were real enough at times; but the poorest Jewish craftsman, pedlar, landlord's steward or petty cleric was immeasurably better off than a

serf. This was particularly true in those European countries where serfdom persisted into the 19th century, whether in a partial or extreme form: Prussia, Austria (including Hungary), Poland and the Polish lands taken by Russia. And it is not without significance that, prior to the beginning of the great Jewish migration of modern times (around 1880), a large majority of all Jews were living in those areas and that their most important social function there was to mediate the oppression of the peasants on behalf of the nobility and the Crown.

Everywhere, classical Judaism developed hatred and contempt for agriculture as an occupation and for peasants as a class, even more than for other Gentiles – a hatred of which I know no parallel in other societies. This is immediately apparent to anyone who is familiar with the Yiddish or Hebrew literature of the 19th and 20th centuries.[9]

Most east-European Jewish socialists (that is, members of exclusively or predominantly Jewish parties and factions) are guilty of never pointing out this fact; indeed, many were themselves tainted with a ferocious anti-peasant attitude inherited from classical Judaism. Of course, zionist 'socialists' were the worst in this respect, but others, such as the Bund, were not much better. A typical example is their opposition to the formation of peasant co-operatives promoted by the Catholic clergy, on the ground that this was 'an act of antisemitism'. This attitude is by no means dead even now; it could be seen very clearly in the racist views held by many Jewish 'dissidents' in the USSR regarding the Russian people, and also in the lack of discussion of this background by so many Jewish socialists, such as Isaac Deutscher. The whole racist propaganda on the theme of the supposed superiority of Jewish morality and intellect (in which many Jewish socialists were prominent) is bound up with a lack of sensitivity for the suffering of that major part of humanity who were especially oppressed during the last thousand years – the peasants.

2 *Classical Jewish society was particularly dependent on kings or on nobles with royal powers.* In the next chapter we discuss various Jewish laws directed against Gentiles, and in particular laws which command Jews to revile Gentiles and refrain from praising them or their customs. These laws allow one and only one exception: a Gentile king, or a locally powerful magnate (in Hebrew *paritz*, in Yiddish *pooretz*). A king is praised and prayed for, and he is obeyed not only in most civil matters but also in some religious ones. As we shall see Jewish doctors, who are in general forbidden to save the lives of ordinary Gentiles on the Sabbath, are commanded to do their utmost in healing magnates and rulers; this partly explains

why kings and noblemen, popes and bishops often employed Jewish physicians. But not only physicians. Jewish tax and customs collectors, or (in eastern Europe) bailiffs of manors could be depended upon to do their utmost for the king or baron, in a way that a Christian could not always be.

The legal status of a Jewish community in the period of classical Judaism was normally based on a 'privilege' – a charter granted by a king or prince (or, in Poland after the 16th century, by a powerful nobleman) to the Jewish community and conferring on it the rights of autonomy – that is, investing the rabbis with the power to dictate to the other Jews. An important part of such privileges, going as far back as the late Roman Empire, is the creation of a Jewish clerical estate which, exactly like the Christian clergy in medieval times, is *exempt from paying taxes to the sovereign* and is allowed to impose taxes on the people under its control – the Jews – for its own benefit. It is interesting to note that this deal between the late Roman Empire and the rabbis antedates by at least one hundred years the very similar privileges granted by Constantine the Great and his successors to the Christian clergy.

From about AD 200 until the early 5th century, the legal position of Jewry in the Roman Empire was as follows. A hereditary Jewish Patriarch (residing in Tiberias in Palestine) was recognised both as a high dignitary in the official hierarchy of the Empire and as supreme chief of all the Jews in the Empire.[10] As a Roman official, the Patriarch was *vir illustris*, of the same high official class which included the consuls, the top military commanders of the Empire and the chief ministers around the throne (the Sacred Consistory), and was out-ranked only by the imperial family. In fact, the Illustrious Patriarch (as he is invariably styled in imperial decrees) out-ranked the provincial governor of Palestine. Emperor Theodosius I, the Great, a pious and orthodox Christian, executed his governor of Palestine for insulting the Patriarch.

At the same time, all the rabbis – who had to be designated by the Patriarch – were freed from the most oppressive Roman taxes and received many official privileges, such as exemption from serving on town councils (which was also one of the first privileges later granted to the Christian clergy). In addition, the Patriarch was empowered to tax the Jews and to discipline them by imposing fines, flogging and other punishments. He used this power in order to suppress Jewish heresies and (as we know from the Talmud) to persecute Jewish preachers who accused him of taxing the Jewish poor for his personal benefit.

We know from Jewish sources that the tax-exempt rabbis

used excommunication and other means within their power to enhance the religious hegemony of the Patriarch. We also hear, mostly indirectly, of the hate and scorn that many of the Jewish peasants and urban poor in Palestine had for the rabbis, as well as of the contempt of the rabbis for the Jewish poor (usually expressed as contempt for the 'ignorant'). Nevertheless, this typical colonial arrangement continued, as it was backed by the might of the Roman Empire.

Similar arrangements existed, within each country, during the whole period of classical Judaism. Their social effects on the Jewish communities differed, however, according to the size of each community. Where there were few Jews, there was normally little social differentiation within the community, which tended to be composed of rich and middle-class Jews, most of whom had considerable rabbinical-talmudic education. But in countries where the number of Jews increased and a big class of Jewish poor appeared, the same cleavage as the one described above manifested itself, and we observe the rabbinical class, in alliance with the Jewish rich, oppressing the Jewish poor in its own interest as well as in the interest of the state – that is, of the Crown and the nobility.

This was, in particular, the situation in pre-1795 Poland. The specific circumstances of Polish Jewry will be outlined below. Here I only want to point out that because of the formation of a large Jewish community in that country, a deep cleavage between the Jewish upper class (the rabbis and the rich) and the Jewish masses developed there from the 18th century and continued throughout the 19th century. So long as the Jewish community had power over its members, the incipient revolts of the poor, who had to bear the main brunt of taxation, were suppressed by the combined force of the naked coercion of Jewish 'self-rule' and religious sanction.

Because of all this, throughout the classical period (as well as in modern times) the rabbis were the most loyal, not to say zealous, supporters of the powers that be; and the more reactionary the regime, the more rabbinical support it had.

3 *The society of classical Judaism is in total opposition to the surrounding non-Jewish society, except the king (or the nobles, when they take over the state).* This is amply illustrated in Chapter 5.

The consequences of these three social features, taken together, go a long way towards explaining the history of classical Jewish communities both in Christian and in Muslim countries.

The position of the Jews is particularly favourable under strong regimes which have retained a feudal character, and in which national consciousness, even at a rudimentary level, has not yet begun to develop. It is even more favourable in countries such as pre-1795 Poland or in the Iberian kingdoms before the latter half of the 15th century, where the formation of a nationally based powerful feudal monarchy was temporarily or permanently arrested. In fact, classical Judaism flourishes best under strong regimes which are dissociated from most classes in society, and in such regimes the Jews fulfil one of the functions of a middle class – but in a permanently dependent form. For this reason they are opposed not only by the peasantry (whose opposition is then unimportant, except for the occasional and rare popular revolt) but more importantly by the non-Jewish middle class (which was on the rise in Europe), and by the plebeian part of the clergy; and they are protected by the upper clergy and the nobility. But in those countries where, feudal anarchy having been curbed, the nobility enters into partnership with the king (and with at least part of the bourgeoisie) to rule the state, which assumes a national or proto-national form, the position of the Jews deteriorates.

This general scheme, valid for Muslim and Christian countries alike, will now be illustrated briefly by a few examples.

England, France and Italy

Since the first period of Jewish residence in England was so brief, and coincided with the development of the English national feudal monarchy, this country can serve as the best illustration of the above scheme. Jews were brought over to England by William the Conqueror, as part of the French-speaking Norman ruling class, with the primary duty of granting loans to those lords, spiritual and temporal, who were otherwise unable to pay their feudal dues (which were particularly heavy in England and more rigorously exacted in that period than in any other European monarchy). Their greatest royal patron was Henry II, and the Magna Carta marked the beginning of their decline, which continued during the conflict of the barons with Henry III. The temporary resolution of this conflict by Edward I, with the formation of Parliament and of 'ordinary' and fixed taxation, was accompanied by the expulsion of the Jews.

Similarly, in France the Jews flourished during the formation of the strong feudal principalities in the 11th and 12th centuries, including the Royal Domain; and their best protector among the Capetian kings was Louis VII (1137–80), notwithstanding his deep and sincere Christian piety. At that time the Jews of France counted themselves as knights (in Hebrew, *parashim*) and the leading Jewish authority in France, Rabbenu Tam, warns them never to accept an invitation by a feudal lord to settle on his domain, unless they are accorded privileges similar to those of other knights. The decline in their position begins with Philip II Augustus, originator of the political and military alliance of the Crown with the rising urban *commune* movement, and plummets under Philip IV the Handsome, who convoked the first Estates General for the whole of France in order to gain support against the pope. The final expulsion of Jews from the whole of France is closely bound up with the firm establishment of the Crown's rights of taxation and the national character of the monarchy.

Similar examples can be given from other European countries where Jews were living during that period. Reserving Christian Spain and Poland for a more detailed discussion, we remark that in Italy, where many city states had a republican form of power, the same regularity is discernible. Jews flourished especially in the Papal States, in the twin feudal kingdoms of Sicily and Naples (until their expulsion, on Spanish orders, *circa* 1500) and in the feudal enclaves of Piedmont. But in the great commercial and independent cities such as Florence their number was small and their social role unimportant.

The Muslim World

The same general scheme applies to Jewish communities during the classical period in Muslim countries as well, except for the important fact that expulsion of Jews, being contrary to Islamic law, was virtually unknown there. (Medieval Catholic canon law, on the other hand, neither commands nor forbids such expulsion.)

Jewish communities flourished in the famous, but socially misinterpreted, Jewish Golden Age in Muslim countries under regimes which were particularly dissociated from the great majority of the people they ruled, and whose power rested on nothing but naked force and a mercenary army. The best example is Muslim Spain, where the very real Jewish Golden Age (of Hebrew poetry, grammar, philosophy etc) begins precisely with the fall of the Spanish Umayyad caliphate after the death of the *de facto* ruler, al-Mansur, in 1002, and the establishment of the numerous *ta'ifa* (faction) kingdoms, all based on naked force. The rise of the famous Jewish commander-in-chief and prime minister of the kingdom of Granada, Samuel the Chief (Shmu'el Hannagid, died 1056), who was also one of the greatest Hebrew poets of all ages, was based primarily on the fact that the kingdom which he served was a tyranny of a rather small Berber military force over the Arabic-speaking inhabitants. A similar situation obtained in the other *ta'ifa*

Arab-Spanish kingdoms. The position of the Jews declined somewhat with the establishment of the Almoravid regime (in 1086–90) and became quite precarious under the strong and popular Almohad regime (after 1147) when, as a result of persecutions, the Jews migrated to the Christian Spanish kingdoms, where the power of the kings was still very slight.

Similar observations can be made regarding the states of the Muslim East. The first state in which the Jewish community reached a position of important political influence was the Fatimid empire, especially after the conquest of Egypt in 969, *because* it was based on the rule of an Isma'ili-shi'ite religious minority. The same phenomenon can be observed in the Seljuk states – based on feudal-type armies, mercenaries and, increasingly, on slave troops (*mamluks*) – and in their successor states. The favour of Saladin to the Jewish communities, first in Egypt, then in other parts of this expanding empire, was based not only on his real personal qualities of tolerance, charity and deep political wisdom, but equally on his rise to power as a rebellious commander of mercenaries freshly arrived in Egypt and then as usurper of the power of the dynasty which he and his father and uncle before him had served.

But perhaps the best Islamic example is the state where the Jews' position was better than anywhere else in the East since the fall of the ancient Persian empire – the Ottoman empire, particularly during its heyday in the 16th century.[11] As is well known, the Ottoman regime was based initially on the almost complete exclusion of the Turks themselves (not to mention other Muslims by birth) from positions of political power and from the most important part of the army, the Janissary corps, both of which were manned by the sultan's Christian-born slaves, abducted in childhood and educated in special schools. Until the end of the 16th century no free-born Turk could become a Janissary or hold any important government office. In such a regime, the role of the Jews in their sphere was quite analogous to that of the Janissaries in theirs. Thus the position of the Jews was best under a regime which was politically most dissociated from the peoples it ruled. With the admission of the Turks themselves (as well as some other Muslim peoples, such as the Albanians) to the ruling class of the Ottoman empire, the position of the Jews declines. However, this decline was not very sharp, because of the continuing arbitrariness and non-national character of the Ottoman regime.

This point is very important, in my opinion, because the relatively good situation of Jews under Islam in general, and under certain Islamic regimes in particular, is used by many Palestinian and other Arab propagandists in a very ignorant, albeit perhaps well-meaning, way. First, they generalise and reduce serious questions of politics and history to mere slogans. Granted that the position of Jews was, *on average*, much better under Islam than under Christianity – the important question to ask is, under *what regimes* was it better or worse? We have seen where such an analysis leads.

But, secondly and more importantly: in a pre-modern state, a 'better' position of the Jewish community normally entailed a greater degree of tyranny exercised within this community by the rabbis against other Jews. To give one example: certainly, the figure of Saladin is one which, considering his period, inspires profound respect. But together with this respect, I for one cannot forget that the enhanced privileges he granted to the Jewish community in Egypt and his appointment of Maimonides as their Chief (*Nagid*) immediately unleashed severe religious persecution of Jewish 'sinners' by the rabbis. For instance, Jewish 'priests' (supposed descendants of the ancient priests who had served in the Temple) are forbidden to marry not only prostitutes[12] but also divorcees. This latter prohibition, which has always caused difficulties, was infringed during the anarchy under the last Fatimid rulers (*circa* 1130–80) by such 'priests' who, contrary to Jewish religious law, were married to Jewish divorcees in Islamic courts (which are nominally empowered to marry non-Muslims). The greater tolerance towards 'the Jews' instituted by Saladin upon his accession to power enabled Maimonides to issue orders to the rabbinical courts in Egypt to seize all Jews who had gone through such forbidden marriages and have them flogged until they 'agreed' to divorce their wives.[13] Similarly, in the Ottoman empire the powers of the rabbinical courts were very great and consequently most pernicious. Therefore the position of Jews in Muslim countries in the past should never be used as a political argument in contemporary (or future) contexts.

Christian Spain

I have left to the last a discussion of the two countries where the position of the Jewish community and the internal development of classical Judaism were most important – Christian Spain[14] (or rather the Iberian peninsula, including Portugal) and pre-1795 Poland.

Politically, the position of Jews in the Christian Spanish kingdoms was the highest ever attained by Jews in any country (except some of the *ta'ifas* and under the Fatimids) before the 19th century. Many Jews served officially as Treasurers General to the kings of Castile, regional and general tax collectors, diplomats (representing their king in foreign courts, both Muslim and Christian, even outside Spain), courtiers and advisers to rulers and great noblemen. And in no other country except Poland did the Jewish community wield such great legal powers over the Jews or used them so widely and publicly, including the power to inflict capital punishment. From the 11th century the persecution of Karaites (a heretical Jewish sect) by flogging them to death if unrepentant was common in Castile. Jewish women who cohabited with Gentiles had their noses cut off by rabbis who explained that 'in this way she will lose her beauty and her non-Jewish lover will come to hate her'. Jews who had the effrontery to attack a rabbinical judge had their hands cut off. Adulterers were imprisoned, after being made to run the gauntlet through the Jewish quarter. In religious disputes, those thought to be heretics had their tongues cut out.

Historically, all this was associated with feudal anarchy and with the attempt of a few 'strong' kings to rule through sheer force, disregarding the parliamentary institutions, the Cortes, which had already come into existence. In this struggle, not only the political and financial power of the Jews but also their military power (at least in the most important kingdom, Castile) was very significant. One example will suffice: both feudal misgovernment and Jewish political influence in Castile reached their peak under Pedro I, justly nick–named the Cruel. The Jewish communities of Toledo, Burgos and many other cities served practically as his garrisons in the long civil war between him and his half-brother, Henry of Trastamara, who after his victory became Henry II (1369–79).[15] The same Pedro I gave the Jews of Castile the right to establish a country-wide inquisition against Jewish religious deviants – more than one hundred years before the establishment of the more famous Catholic Holy Inquisition.

As in other western European countries, the gradual emergence of national consciousness around the monarchy, which began under the house of Trastamara and after ups and downs reached a culmination under the Catholic Kings Ferdinand and Isabella, was accompanied first by a decline in the position of the Jews, then by popular movements and pressures against them and finally by their expulsion. On the whole the Jews were defended by the nobility and upper clergy. It was the more plebeian sections of the church, particularly the mendicant orders, involved in the life of the lower classes, which were hostile to them. The great enemies of the Jews, Torquemada and Cardinal Ximenes, were also great reformers of the Spanish church, making it much less corrupt and much more dependent on the monarchy instead of being the preserve of the feudal aristocracy.

Poland

The old pre-1795 Poland – a feudal republic with an elective king – is a converse example; it illustrates how before the advent of the modern state the position of the Jews was socially most important, and their internal autonomy greatest, under a regime which was completely retarded to the point of utter degeneracy.

Due to many causes, medieval Poland lagged in its development behind countries like England and France; a strong feudal-type monarchy – yet without any parliamentary institutions – was formed there only in the 14th century, especially under Casimir the Great (1333–70). Immediately after his death, changes of dynasty and other factors led to a very rapid development of the power of the noble magnates, then also of the petty nobility, so that by 1572 the process of reduction of the king to a figure head and exclusion of all other non-noble estates from political power was virtually complete. In the following two hundred years, the lack of government turned into an acknowledged anarchy, to the point where a court decision in a case affecting a nobleman was only a legal licence to wage a private war to enforce the verdict (for there was no other way to enforce it) and where feuds between great noble houses in the 18th century involved private armies numbering tens of thousands, much larger than the derisory forces of the official army of the Republic.

This process was accompanied by a debasement in the position of the Polish peasants (who had been free in the early Middle Ages) to the point of utter serfdom, hardly distinguishable from outright slavery and certainly the worst in Europe. The desire of noblemen in neighbouring countries to enjoy the power of the Polish *pan* over his peasants (including the power of life and death without any right of appeal) was instrumental in the territorial expansion of Poland. The situation in the 'eastern' lands of Poland (Byelorussia and the Ukraine) – colonised and settled by newly enserfed peasants – was worst of all.[16]

A small number of Jews (albeit in important positions) had apparently been living in Poland since the creation of the Polish state. A significant Jewish immigration into that country began in the 13th century and increased under Casimir the Great, with the decline in the Jewish position in western and then in central Europe. Not very much is known about Polish

Jewry in that period. But with the decline of the monarchy in the 16th century – particularly under Sigismund I the Old (1506–48) and his son Sigismund II Augustus (1548–72) – Polish Jewry burst into social and political prominence accompanied, as usual, with a much greater degree of autonomy. It was at this time that Poland's Jews were granted their greatest privileges, culminating in the establishment of the famous Committee of Four Lands, a very effective autonomous Jewish organ of rule and jurisdiction over all the Jews in Poland's four divisions. One of its many important functions was to collect all the taxes from Jews all over the country, deducting part of the yield for its own use and for the use of local Jewish communities, and passing the rest on to the state treasury.

What was the social role of Polish Jewry from the beginning of the 16th century until 1795? With the decline of royal power, the king's usual role in relation to the Jews was rapidly taken over by the nobility – with lasting and tragic results both for the Jews themselves and for the common people of the Polish republic. All over Poland the nobles used Jews as their agents to undermine the commercial power of the Royal Towns, which were weak in any case. Alone among the countries of western Christendom, in Poland a nobleman's property inside a Royal Town was exempt from the town's laws and guild regulations. In most cases the nobles settled their Jewish clients in such properties, thus giving rise to a lasting conflict. The Jews were usually 'victorious', in the sense that the towns could neither subjugate nor drive them off; but in the frequent popular riots Jewish lives (and, even more, Jewish property) were lost. The nobles still got the profits. Similar or worse consequences followed from the frequent use of Jews as commercial agents of noblemen: they won exemption from most Polish tolls and tariffs, to the loss of the native bourgeoisie.

But the most lasting and tragic results occurred in the eastern provinces of Poland – roughly, the area east of the present border, including almost the whole of the present Ukraine and reaching up to the Great-Russian language frontier. (Until 1667 the Polish border was far east of the Dnieper, so that Poltava, for example, was inside Poland.) In those wide territories there were hardly any Royal Towns. The towns were established by nobles and belonged to them – and they were settled almost exclusively by Jews. Until 1939, the population of many Polish towns east of the river Bug was at least 90 per cent Jewish, and this demographic phenomenon was even more pronounced in that area of Tsarist Russia annexed from Poland and known as the Jewish Pale. Outside the towns very many Jews throughout Poland, but especially in the east, were employed as the direct supervisors and oppressors of the enserfed peasantry – as bailiffs of whole manors (invested with the landlord's full coercive powers) or as lessees of particular feudal monopolies such as the corn mill, the liquor still and public house (with the right of armed search of peasant houses for illicit stills) or the bakery, and as collectors of customary feudal dues of all kinds. In short, in eastern Poland, under the rule of the nobles (and of the feudalised church, formed exclusively from the nobility) the Jews were both the *immediate exploiters of the peasantry* and virtually the only town-dwellers.

No doubt, most of the profit they extracted from the peasants was passed on to the landlords, in one way or another. No doubt, the oppression and subjugation of the Jews by the nobles were severe, and the historical record tells many a harrowing tale of the hardship and humiliation inflicted by noblemen on 'their' Jews. But, as we have remarked, the peasants suffered worse oppression at the hands of *both* landlords and Jews; and one may assume that, except in times of peasant uprisings, the full weight of the Jewish religious laws against Gentiles fell upon the peasants. As will be seen in the next chapter, these laws are suspended or mitigated in cases where it is feared that they might arouse dangerous hostility towards Jews; but the hostility of the peasants could be disregarded as ineffectual so long as the Jewish bailiff could shelter under the 'peace' of a great lord.

The situation stagnated until the advent of the modern state, by which time Poland had been dismembered. Therefore Poland was the only big country in western Christendom from which the Jews were never expelled. A new middle class could not arise out of the utterly enslaved peasantry; and the old bourgeoisie was geographically limited and commercially weak, and therefore powerless. Overall, matters got steadily worse, but without any substantial change.

Internal conditions within the Jewish community moved in a similar course. In the period 1500–1795, one of the most superstition-ridden in the history of Judaism, Polish Jewry was the most superstitious and fanatic of all Jewish communities. The considerable power of the Jewish autonomy was used increasingly to stifle all original or innovative thought, to promote the most shameless exploitation of the Jewish poor by the Jewish rich in alliance with the rabbis, and to justify the Jews' role in the oppression of the peasants in the service of the nobles. Here, too, there was no way out except by liberation from the outside. Pre-1795 Poland, where the *social* role of the Jews was more important than in any other classical diaspora, illustrates better than any other country the bankruptcy of classical Judaism.

Anti-Jewish Persecutions

During the whole period of classical Judaism, Jews were often subjected to persecutions[17] – and this fact now serves as the main 'argument' of the apologists of the Jewish religion with its anti-Gentile laws and especially of zionism. Of course, the Nazi extermination of five to six million European Jews is supposed to be the crowning argument in that line. We must therefore consider this phenomenon and its contemporary aspect. This is particularly important in view of the fact that the descendants of the Jews of pre-1795 Poland (often called 'east-European Jews' – as opposed to Jews from the German cultural domain of the early 19th century, including the present Austria, Bohemia and Moravia) now wield predominant political power in Israel as well as in the Jewish communities in the USA and other English-speaking countries; and, because of their particular past history, this mode of thinking is especially entrenched among them, much more than among other Jews.

We must, first, draw a sharp distinction between the persecutions of Jews during the classical period on the one hand, and the Nazi extermination on the other. The former were popular movements, coming from below; whereas the latter was inspired, organised and carried out from above: indeed, by state officials. Such acts as the Nazi state-organised extermination are relatively rare in human history, although other cases do exist (the extermination of the Tasmanians and several other colonial peoples, for example). Moreover, the Nazis intended to wipe out other peoples besides the Jews: Gypsies were exterminated like Jews, and the extermination of Slavs was well under way, with the systematic massacre of millions of civilians and prisoners of war. However, it is the recurrent persecution of Jews in so many countries during the classical period which is the model (and the excuse) for the zionist politicians in their persecution of the Palestinians, as well as the argument used by apologists of Judaism in general; and it is this phenomenon which we consider now.

It must be pointed out that in all the worst anti-Jewish persecutions, that is, where Jews were killed, the ruling elite – the emperor and the pope, the kings, the higher aristocracy and the upper clergy, as well as the rich bourgeoisie in the autonomous cities – were always on the side of the Jews. The latter's enemies belonged to the more oppressed and exploited classes and those close to them in daily life and interests, such as the friars of the mendicant orders.[18] It is true that in most (but I think not in all) cases members of the elite defended the Jews neither out of considerations of humanity nor because of sympathy to the Jews as such, but for the type of reason used generally by rulers in justification of their interests – the fact that the Jews were useful and profitable (to them), defence of 'law and order', hatred of the lower classes and fear that anti-Jewish riots might develop into general popular rebellion. Still, the fact remains that they did defend the Jews. For this reason all the massacres of Jews during the classical period were part of a peasant rebellion or other popular movements at times when the government was for some reason especially weak. This is true even in the partly exceptional case of Tsarist Russia. The Tsarist government, acting surreptitiously through its secret police, did promote pogroms; but it did so only when it was particularly weak (after the assassination of Alexander II in 1881, and in the period immediately before and after the 1905 revolution) and even then took care to contain the breakdown of 'law and order'. During the time of its greatest strength – for example, under Nicholas I or in the latter part of the reign of Alexander III, when the opposition had been smashed – pogroms were not tolerated by the Tsarist regime, although *legal* discrimination against Jews was intensified.

The general rule can be observed in all the major massacres of Jews in Christian Europe. During the first crusade, it was not the proper armies of the knights, commanded by famous dukes and counts, which molested the Jews, but the spontaneous popular hosts composed almost exclusively of peasants and paupers in the wake of Peter the Hermit. In each city the bishop or the emperor's representative opposed them and tried, often in vain, to protect the Jews.[19] The anti-Jewish riots in England which accompanied the third crusade were part of a popular movement directed also against royal officials, and some rioters were punished by Richard I. The massacres of Jews during the outbreaks of the Black Death occurred against the strict orders of the pope, the emperor, the bishops and the German princes. In the free towns, for example in Strasbourg, they were usually preceded by a local revolution in which the oligarchic town council, which protected the Jews, was overthrown and replaced by a more popular one. The great 1391 massacres of Jews in Spain took place under a feeble regency government and at a time when the papacy, weakened by the Great Schism between competing popes, was unable to control the mendicant friars.

Perhaps the most outstanding example is the great massacre of Jews during the Chmielnicki revolt in the Ukraine (1648), which started as a mutiny of Cossack officers but soon turned into a widespread popular movement of the oppressed serfs: 'The unprivileged, the subjects, the Ukrainians, the Orthodox [persecuted by the Polish Catholic church] were rising against their Catholic Polish masters, particularly against their masters' bailiffs, clergy and Jews.'[20] This *typical* peasant uprising against extreme oppression, an uprising accompanied not only by massacres committed by the rebels but also by even more horrible atrocities and 'counter-terror' of the Polish magnates' private armies,[21] has remained emblazoned in the consciousness of east-European Jews to this very day – not, however, as a peasant uprising, a revolt of the oppressed, of the real wretched of the earth, nor even as a vengeance visited upon *all* the servants of the Polish nobility, but as an act of gratuitous antisemitism directed against Jews as such. In fact, the voting of the Ukrainian delegation at the UN and, more generally, Soviet policies on the Middle East, are often 'explained' in the Israeli press as 'a heritage of Chmielnicki' or of his 'descendants'.

Modern Antisemitism

The character of anti-Jewish persecutions underwent a radical change in modern times. With the advent of the modern state, the abolition of serfdom and the achievement of minimal individual rights, the special socio-economic function of the Jews necessarily disappears. Along with it disappear also the powers of the Jewish community over its members; individual Jews in growing numbers win the freedom to enter the general society of their countries. Naturally, this transition aroused a violent reaction both on the part of Jews (especially their rabbis) and of those elements in European society who opposed the open society and for whom the whole process of liberation of the individual was anathema.

Modern antisemitism appears first in France and Germany, then in Russia, after about 1870. Contrary to the prevalent opinion among Jewish socialists, I do not believe that its beginnings or its subsequent development until the present day can be ascribed to 'capitalism'. On the contrary, in my opinion the successful capitalists in all countries were on the whole remarkably free from antisemitism, and the countries in which capitalism was established first and in its most extensive form – such as England and Belgium – were also those where antisemitism was far less widespread than elsewhere.[22]

Early modern antisemitism (1880–1900) was a reaction of bewildered men, who deeply hated modern society in all its aspects, both good and bad, and who were ardent believers in the conspiracy theory of history. The Jews were cast in the role of scapegoat for the breakup of the old society (which anti-semitic nostalgia imagined as even more closed and ordered than it had ever been in reality) and 'for all that was disturbing in modern times. But right at the start the antisemites were faced with what was, for them, a difficult problem: how to define this scapegoat, particularly in popular terms? What is to be the supposed common denominator of the Jewish musician, banker, craftsman and beggar – especially after the common religious features had largely dissolved, at least externally? The 'theory' of the Jewish race was the modern antisemitic answer to this problem.

In contrast, the old Christian, and even more so Muslim opposition to classical Judaism was remarkably free from rac-ism. No doubt this was to some extent a consequence of the universal character of Christianity and Islam, as well as of their original connection with Judaism (St Thomas More repeatedly rebuked a woman who objected when he told her that the Virgin Mary was Jewish). But in my opinion a far more impor-tant reason was the social role of the Jews as an integral part of the upper classes. In many countries Jews were treated as potential nobles and, upon conversion, were able immediately to intermarry with the highest nobility. The nobility of 15th cen-tury Castile and Aragon or the aristocracy of 18th century Poland – to take the two cases where intermarriage with con-verted Jews was widespread – would hardly be likely to marry Spanish peasants or Polish serfs, no matter how much praise the Gospel has for the poor.

It is the modern myth of the Jewish 'race' – of outwardly hidden but supposedly dominant characteristics of 'the Jews', independent of history, of social role, of anything – which is the formal and most important distinguishing mark of modern antisemitism. This was in fact perceived by some Church lead-ers when modern antisemitism first appeared as a movement of some strength. Some French Catholic leaders, for example, opposed the new racist doctrine expounded by E. Drumont, the first popular modern French antisemite and author of the noto-rious book *La France Juive* (1886), which achieved wide circula-tion.[23] Early modern German antisemites encountered similar opposition.

It must be pointed out that some important groups of European conservatives were quite prepared to play along with modern antisemitism and use it for their own ends, and the antisemites were equally ready to use the conservatives when the occasion offered itself, although at bottom there was little similarity between the two parties. 'The victims who were most harshly treated [by the pen of the above-mentioned Drumont] were not the Rothschilds but the great nobles who courted them. Drumont did not spare the Royal Family ... or the bishops, or for that matter the Pope.'[24] Nevertheless, many of the French great nobles, bishops and conservatives generally were quite happy to use Drumont and antisemitism during the crisis of the Dreyfus affair in an attempt to bring down the republican regime.

This type of opportunistic alliance reappeared many times in various European countries until the defeat of Nazism. The conservatives' hatred of radicalism and especially of all forms of socialism blinded many of them to the nature of their political bedfellows. In many cases they were literally prepared to ally themselves with the devil, forgetting the old saying that one needs a very long spoon to sup with him.

The effectiveness of modern antisemitism, and of its alliance with conservatism, depended on several factors.

First, the older tradition of Christian religious opposition to Jews, which existed in many (though by no means all) European countries, could, if supported or at least unopposed by the clergy, be harnessed to the antisemitic bandwagon. The actual response of the clergy in each country was largely determined by specific local historical and social circumstances. In the Catholic Church, the tendency for an opportunistic alliance with antisemitism was strong in France but not in Italy; in Poland and Slovakia but not in Bohemia. The Greek Orthodox Church had notorious antisemitic tendencies in Romania but took the opposite line in Bulgaria. Among the Protestant Churches, the German was deeply divided on this issue, others (such as the Latvian and Estonian) tended to be antisemitic, but many (for example the Dutch, Swiss and Scandinavian) were among the earliest to condemn antisemitism.

Secondly, antisemitism was largely a generic expression of xenophobia, a desire for a 'pure' homogeneous society. But in many European countries around 1900 (and in fact until quite recently) the Jew was virtually the only 'stranger'. This was particularly true of Germany. In principle, the German racists of the early 20th century hated and despised Blacks just as much as Jews; but there were no Blacks in Germany then. Hate is of course much more easily focused on the present than on the absent, especially under the conditions of the time, when mass travel and tourism did not exist and most Europeans never left their own country in peacetime.

Thirdly, the successes of the tentative alliance between conservatism and antisemitism were inversely proportional to the power and capabilities of its opponents. And the consistent and effective opponents of antisemitism in Europe are the political forces of liberalism and socialism – historically the same forces that continue in various ways the tradition symbolised by the War of Dutch Independence (1568–1648), the English Revolution and the Great French Revolution. On the European continent the main shibboleth is the attitude towards the Great French Revolution – roughly speaking, those who are for it are against antisemitism; those who accept it with regret would be at least prone to an alliance with the antisemites; those who hate it and would like to undo its achievements are the milieu from which antisemitism develops.

Nevertheless, a sharp distinction must be made between conservatives and even reactionaries on the one hand and actual racists and antisemites on the other. Modern racism (of which antisemitism is part) although caused by specific social conditions, becomes, when it gains strength, a force that in my opinion can only be described as demonic. After coming to power, and for its duration, I believe it defies analysis by any presently understood social theory or set of merely social observations – and in particular by any known theory invoking interests, be they class or state interests, or other than purely psychological 'interests' of any entity that can be defined in the present state of human knowledge. But this I do not mean that such forces are unknowable in principle; on the contrary, one must hope that with the growth of human knowledge they will come to be understood. But at present they are neither understood nor capable of being rationally predicted – and this applies to all racism in all societies.[25] As a matter of fact, no political figure or group of any political colour in any country had predicted even vaguely the horrors of Nazism. Only artists and poets such as Heine were able to glimpse some of what the future had in store. We do not know how they did it; and besides, many of their other hunches were wrong.

The Zionist Response

Historically, zionism is both a reaction to antisemitism and a conservative alliance with it – although the zionists, like other European conservatives, did not fully realise with whom they were allying themselves.

Until the rise of modern antisemitism, the mood of European Jewry was optimistic, indeed excessively so. This was manifested not only in the very large number of Jews, particularly in western countries, who simply opted out of classical Judaism, apparently without any great regret, in the first or second generation after this became possible, but also in the formation of a strong cultural movement, the Jewish Enlightenment (*Haskalah*), which began in Germany and Austria around 1780, was then carried into eastern Europe and by 1850–70 was making itself felt as a considerable social force. I cannot enter here into a discussion of the movement's cultural achievements, such as the revival of Hebrew literature and the creation of a wonderful literature in Yiddish. However, it is important to note that despite many internal differences, the movement as a whole was characterised by two common beliefs: a belief in the need for a fundamental critique of Jewish society and particularly of the social role of the Jewish religion in its classical form, and the almost messianic hope for the victory of the 'forces of good' in European societies. The latter forces were naturally defined by the sole criterion of their support for Jewish emancipation.

The growth of antisemitism as a popular movement, and the many alliances of the conservative forces with it, dealt a severe blow to the Jewish Enlightenment. The blow was especially devastating because in actual fact the rise of antisemitism occurred just after the Jews were emancipated in some European countries, and even before they were freed in others. The Jews of the Austrian empire received fully equal rights only in 1867. In Germany, some independent states emancipated their Jews quite early, but others did not; notably, Prussia was grudging and tardy in this matter, and final emancipation of the Jews in the German empire as a whole was only granted by Bismarck in 1871. In the Ottoman empire the Jews were subject to official discrimination until 1909, and in Russia (as well as Romania) until 1917. Thus modern antisemitism began within a decade of the emancipation of the Jews in central Europe and long before the emancipation of the biggest Jewish community at that time, that of the Tsarist empire.

It is therefore easy for the zionists to ignore half of the relevant facts, revert to the segregationist stance of classical Judaism, and claim that since all Gentiles always hate and persecute all Jews, the only solution would be to remove all the Jews bodily and concentrate them in Palestine or Uganda or wherever.[26] Some early Jewish critics of zionism were quick to point out that if one assumes a permanent and ahistorical incompatibility between Jews and Gentiles – an assumption shared by both zionists and antisemites! – then to concentrate the Jews in one place would simply bring upon them the hatred of the Gentiles in that part of the world (as indeed was to happen, though for very different reasons). But as far as I know this logical argument did not make any impression, just as all the logical and factual arguments against the myth of the 'Jewish race' made not the slightest difference to the antisemites.

In fact, close relations have always existed between zionists and antisemites: exactly like some of the European conservatives, the zionists thought they could ignore the 'demonic' character of antisemitism and use the antisemites for their own purposes. Many examples of such alliances are well known. Herzl allied himself with the notorious Count von Plehve, the antisemitic minister of Tsar Nicholas II;[27] Jabotinsky made a pact with Petlyura, the reactionary Ukrainian leader whose forces massacred some 100,000 Jews in 1918–21; Ben-Gurion's allies among the French extreme right during the Algerian war included some notorious antisemites who were, however, careful to explain that they were only against the Jews in France, not in Israel.

Perhaps the most shocking example of this type is the delight with which some zionist leaders in Germany welcomed Hitler's rise to power, because they shared his belief in the primacy of 'race' and his hostility to the assimilation of Jews among 'Aryans'. They congratulated Hitler on his triumph over the common enemy – the forces of liberalism. Dr Joachim Prinz, a zionist rabbi who subsequently emigrated to the USA, where he rose to be vice-chairman of the World Jewish Congress and a leading light in the World Zionist Organization (as well as a great friend of Golda Meir), published in 1934 a special book, *Wir Juden* (We, Jews), to celebrate Hitler's so-called German Revolution and the defeat of liberalism:

> The meaning of the German Revolution for the German nation will eventually be clear to those who have created it and formed its image. Its meaning for us must be set forth here: the fortunes of liberalism are lost. The only form of political life which has helped Jewish assimilation is sunk.[28]

The victory of Nazism rules out assimilation and mixed marriages as an option for Jews. 'We are not unhappy about this,' said Dr Prinz. In the fact that Jews are being forced to identify themselves as Jews, he sees 'the fulfilment of our desires'. And further:

> We want assimilation to be replaced by a new law: *the declaration of belonging to the Jewish nation and Jewish race*. A state build upon the principle of the purity of nation and race can only honoured and respected by a Jew who declares his belonging to his own kind. Having so declared himself, he will never be capable of faulty loyalty towards a state. The state cannot want other Jews but such as declare themselves as belonging to their nation. It will not want Jewish flatterers

and crawlers. It must demand of us faith and loyalty to our
own interest. For only he who honours his *own* breed and his
own blood can have an attitude of honour towards the *national will of other nations.*[29]

The whole book is full of similar crude flatteries of Nazi ideology,
glee at the defeat of liberalism and particularly of the ideas of the
French Revolution[30] and great expectations that, in the congenial
atmosphere of the myth of the Aryan race, zionism and the myth
of the Jewish race will also thrive.

Of course, Dr Prinz, like many other early sympathisers
and allies of Nazism, did not realise where that movement
(and modern antisemitism generally) was leading. Equally,
many people at present do not realise where zionism – the
movement in which Dr Prinz was an honoured figure – is
tending: to a combination of all the old hates of classical
Judaism towards Gentiles and to the indiscriminate and ahistorical use of all the persecutions of Jews throughout history
in order to justify the zionist persecution of the Palestinians.

For, insane as it sounds, it is nevertheless plain upon close
examination of the real motives of the zionists, that one of the
most deep-seated ideological sources of the zionist establishment's persistent hostility towards the Palestinians is the fact
that they are identified in the minds of many east-European
Jews with the rebellious east-European peasants who participated in the Chmielnicki uprising and in similar revolts – and
the latter are in turn identified ahistorically with modern antisemitism and Nazism.

Confronting the Past

All Jews who really want to extricate themselves from the
tyranny of the totalitarian Jewish past must face the question
of their attitude towards the *popular* anti-Jewish manifestations
of the past, particularly those connected with the rebellions of
enserfed peasants. On the other side, all the apologists of the
Jewish religion and of Jewish segregationism and chauvinism
also take their stand – both ultimately and in current debates –
on the same question. The undoubted fact that the peasant
revolutionaries committed shocking atrocities against Jews (as
well as against their other oppressors) is used as an 'argument'
by those apologists, in exactly the same way that the Palestinian terror is used to justify the denial of justice to the
Palestinians.

Our own answer must be a universal one, applicable in
principle to *all* comparable cases. And, for a Jew who truly
seeks liberation from Jewish particularism and racism and from

the dead hand of the Jewish religion, such an answer is not very difficult.

After all, revolts of oppressed peasants against their masters and their masters' bailiffs are common in human history. A generation after the Chmielnicki uprising of the Ukrainian peasants, the Russian peasants rose under the leadership of Stenka Razin, and again, one hundred years later, in the Pugachev rebellion. In Germany there was the Peasant War of 1525, in France the Jacquerie of 1357–8 and many other popular revolts, not to mention the many slave uprisings in all parts of the world. All of them – and I have intentionally chosen to mention examples in which Jews were *not* targets – were attended by horrifying massacres, just as the Great French Revolution was accompanied by appalling acts of terror. What is the position of true progressives – and, by now, of most ordinary decent educated people, be they Russian, German or French – on these rebellions? Do decent English historians, even when noting the massacres of Englishmen by rebellious Irish peasants rising against their enslavement, condemn the latter as 'anti-English racists'? What is the attitude of progressive French historians towards the great slave revolution in Santo Domingo, where many French women and children were butchered? To ask the question is to answer it. But to ask a similar question of many 'progressive' or even 'socialist' Jewish circles is to receive a very different answer; here an enslaved peasant is transformed into a racist monster, if Jews profited from his state of slavery and exploitation.

The maxim that those who do not learn from history are condemned to repeat it applies to those Jews who refuse to come to terms with the Jewish past: they have become its slaves and are repeating it in zionist and Israeli policies. The State of Israel now fulfils towards the oppressed peasants of many countries – not only in the Middle East but also far beyond it – a role not unlike that of the Jews in pre-1795 Poland: that of a bailiff to the imperial oppressor. It is characteristic and instructive that Israel's major role in arming the forces of the Somoza regime in Nicaragua, and those of Guatemala, El Salvador, Chile and the rest has not given rise to any wide public debate in Israel or among *organised* Jewish communities in the diaspora. Even the narrower question of expediency – whether the selling of weapons to a dictatorial butcher of freedom fighters and peasants is in the long term interest of Jews – is seldom asked. Even more significant is the large part taken in this business by religious Jews, and the total silence of their rabbis (who are very vocal in inciting hatred against Arabs). It seems that Israel and zionism are a throw-back to the role of classical Judaism – writ large, on a global scale, and under more dangerous circumstances.

The only possible answer to all this, first of all by Jews, must be that given by all true advocates of freedom and humanity in all countries, all peoples and all great philosophies – limited though they sometimes are, as the human condition itself is limited. We must confront the Jewish past and those aspects of the present which are based simultaneously on lying about that past and worshipping it. The prerequisites for this are, first, total honesty about the facts and, secondly, the belief (leading to action, whenever possible) in universalist human principles of ethics and politics.

The ancient Chinese sage Mencius (4th century BC), much admired by Voltaire, once wrote:

> This is why I say that all men have a sense of commiseration: here is a man who suddenly notices a child about to fall into a well. Invariably he will feel a sense of alarm and compassion. And this is not for the purpose of gaining the favour of the child's parents or of seeking the approbation of his neighbours and friends, or for fear of blame should he fail to rescue it. Thus we see that no man is without a sense of compassion or a sense of shame or a sense of courtesy or a sense of right and wrong. The sense of compassion is the beginning of humanity, the sense of shame is the beginning of righteousness, and sense of courtesy is the beginning of decorum, the sense of right and wrong is the beginning of wisdom. Every man has within himself these four beginnings, just as he has four limbs. Since everyone has these four beginnings within him, the man who considers himself incapable of exercising them is destroying himself.

We have seen above, and will show in greater detail in the next chapter how far removed from this are the precepts with which the Jewish religion in its classical and talmudic form is poisoning minds and hearts.

The road to a genuine revolution in Judaism – to making it humane, allowing Jews to understand their own past, thereby re-educating themselves out of its tyranny – lies through an unrelenting critique of the Jewish religion. Without fear or favour, we must speak out against what belongs to our own past as Voltaire did against his:

Écrasez l'infâme!

Chapter 5

The Laws Against Non-Jews

As explained in Chapter 3, the Halakhah, that is the legal system of classical Judaism – as practised by virtually all Jews from the 9th century to the end of the 18th and as maintained to this very day in the form of Orthodox Judaism – is based primarily on the Babylonian Talmud. However, because of the unwieldy complexity of the legal disputations recorded in the Talmud, more manageable codifications of talmudic law became necessary and were indeed compiled by successive generations of rabbinical scholars. Some of these have acquired great authority and are in general use. For this reasons we shall refer for the most part to such compilations (and their most reputable commentaries) rather than directly to the Talmud. It is however correct to assume that the compilation referred to reproduces faithfully the meaning of the talmudic text and the additions made by later scholars on the basis of that meaning.

The earliest code of talmudic law which is still of major importance is the *Mishneh Torah* written by Moses Maimonides in the late 12th century. The most authoritative code, widely used to date as a handbook, is the *Shulhan 'Arukh* composed by R. Yosef Karo in the late 16th century as a popular condensation of his own much more voluminous *Beyt Yosef* which was intended for the advanced scholar. The *Shulhan 'Arukh* is much commented upon; in addition to classical commentaries dating from the 17th century, there is an important 20th century one, *Mishnah Berurah*. Finally, the *Talmudic Encyclopedia* – a modern compilation published in Israel from the 1950s and edited by the country's greatest Orthodox rabbinical scholars – is a good compendium of the whole talmudic literature.

Murder and Genocide

According to the Jewish religion, the murder of a Jew is a capital offence and one of the three most heinous sins (the other two being idolatry and adultery). Jewish religious courts and secular authorities are commanded to punish, even beyond the limits of the ordinary administration of justice, anyone guilty of murdering a Jew. A Jew who indirectly causes the death of another Jew is, however, only guilty of what talmudic law calls a sin against the 'laws of Heaven', to be punished by God rather than by man.

When the victim is a Gentile, the position is quite different. A Jew who murders a Gentile is guilty only of a sin against the laws of Heaven, not punishable by a court.[1] To cause indirectly the death of a Gentile is no sin at all.[2]

Thus, one of the two most important commentators on the *Shulhan 'Arukh* explains that when it comes to a Gentile, 'one must not lift one's hand to harm him, but one may harm him indirectly, for instance by removing a ladder after he had fallen into a crevice ... there is no prohibition here, because it was not done directly.'[3] He points out, however, that an act leading indirectly to a Gentile's death is forbidden if it may cause the spread of hostility towards Jews.[4]

A Gentile murderer who happens to be under Jewish jurisdiction must be executed whether the victim was Jewish or not. However, if the victim was Gentile and the murderer converts to Judaism, he is not punished.[5]

All this has a direct and practical relevance to the realities of the State of Israel. Although the state's criminal laws make no distinction between Jew and Gentile, such distinction is certainly made by Orthodox rabbis, who in guiding their flock follow the Halakhah. Of special importance is the advice they give to religious soldiers.

Since even the minimal interdiction against murdering a Gentile outright applies only to 'Gentiles with whom we [the Jews] are not at war', various rabbinical commentators in the past drew the logical conclusion that in wartime all Gentiles belonging to a hostile population may, or even should be killed.[6] Since 1973 this doctrine is being publicly propagated for the guidance of religious Israeli soldiers. The first such official exhortation was included in a booklet published by the Central Region Command of the Israeli Army, whose area includes the West Bank. In this booklet the Command's Chief Chaplain writes:

> When our forces come across civilians during a war or in hot pursuit or in a raid, so long as there is no certainty that those civilians are incapable of harming our forces, then according to the Halakhah they may and even should be killed ... Under no circumstances should an Arab be trusted, even if he makes an impression of being civilised ... In war, when our forces storm the enemy, they are allowed and even enjoined by the Halakhah to kill even good civilians, that is, civilians who are ostensibly good.[7]

The same doctrine is expounded in the following exchange of letters between a young Israeli soldier and his rabbi, published in the yearbook of one of the country's most prestigious religious colleges, Midrashiyyat No'am, where many leaders and activists of the National Religious Party and Gush Emunim have been educated.[8]

Letter from the soldier Moshe to Rabbi Shim'on Weiser

'With God's help, to His Honour, my dear Rabbi,

'First I would like to ask how you and your family are. I hope all is well. I am, thank God, feeling well. A long time I have not written. Please forgive me. Sometimes I recall the verse "when shall I come and appear before God?"[9] I hope, without being certain, that I shall come during one of the leaves. I must do so.

'In one of the discussions in our group, there was a debate about the "purity of weapons" and we discussed whether it is permitted to kill unarmed men – or women and children. Or perhaps we should take revenge on the Arabs? And then everyone answered according to his own understanding. I could not arrive at a clear decision, whether Arabs should be treated like the Amalekites, meaning that one is permitted to murder [*sic*] them until their remembrance is blotted out from under heaven,[10] or perhaps one should do as in a just war, in which one kills only the soldiers.

'A second problem I have is whether I am permitted to put myself in danger by allowing a woman to stay alive? For there have been cases when women threw hand grenades. Or am I permitted to give water to an Arab who put his hand up? For there may be reason to fear that he only means to deceive me and will kill me, and such things have happened.

'I conclude with a warm greeting to the rabbi and all his family. – *Moshe*.'

Reply of R. Shim'on Weiser to Moshe

'With the help of Heaven. Dear Moshe, Greetings.

'I am starting this letter this evening although I know I cannot finish it this evening, both because I am busy and because I would like to make it a long letter, to answer your questions in full, for which purpose I shall have to copy out some of the sayings of our sages, of blessed memory, and interpret them.[11]

'The non-Jewish nations have a custom according to which war has its own rules, like those of a game, like the rules of football or basketball. But according to the sayings of our sages, of blessed memory, [...] war for us is not a game but a vital necessity, and only by this standard must we decide how to wage it. On the one hand [...] we seem to learn that if a Jew murders a Gentile, he is regarded as a murderer and, except for the fact that no court has the right to punish him, the gravity of the deed is like that of any other murder. But we find in the very same authorities in another place [...] that Rabbi Shim'on used to say: "The best of Gentiles – kill him; the best of snakes – dash out its brains."

'It might perhaps be argued that the expression "kill" in the saying of R. Shim'on is only figurative and should not be taken literally but as meaning "oppress" or some similar attitude, and in this way we also avoid a contradiction with the authorities quoted earlier. Or one might argue that this saying, though meant literally, is [merely] his own personal opinion, disputed by other sages [quoted earlier]. But we find the true explanation in the Tosafot.[12] There [...] we learn the following comment on the talmudic pronouncement that Gentiles who fall into a well should not be helped out, but neither should they be pushed into the well to be killed, which means that they should neither be saved from death nor killed directly. And the Tosafot write as follows: "And if it is queried [because] in another place it was said *The best of Gentiles – kill him*, then the answer is that this [saying] is meant for wartime." [...]

'According to the commentators of the Tosafot, a distinction must be made between wartime and peace, so that although during peace time it is forbidden to kill Gentiles, in a case that occurs in wartime it is a *mitzvah* [imperative, religious duty] to kill them. [...]

'And this is the difference between a Jew and a Gentile: although the rule "Whoever comes to kill you, kill him first" applies to a Jew, as was said in Tractate *Sanhedrin* [of the Talmud], page 72a, still it only applies to him if there is [actual] ground to fear that he is coming to kill you. But a Gentile during wartime is usually to be presumed so, except when it is quite clear that he has no evil intent. This is the rule of "purity of weapons" according to the Halakhah – and not the alien conception which is now accepted in the Israeli army and which has been the cause of many [Jewish] casualties. I enclose a newspaper cutting with the speech made last week in the Knesset by Rabbi Kalman Kahana, which shows in a very lifelike – and also painful – way how this "purity of weapons" has caused deaths.

'I conclude here, hoping that you will not find the length of this letter irksome. This subject was being discussed even without your letter, but your letter caused me to write up the whole matter.

'Be in peace, you and all Jews, and [I hope to] see you soon, as you say. Yours – *Shim'on*.

Reply of Moshe to R. Shim'on Weiser

'To His Honour, my dear Rabbi,

'First I hope that you and your family are in health and are all right.

'I have received your long letter and am grateful for your personal watch over me, for I assume that you write to many, and most of your time is taken up with your studies in your own programme.

'Therefore my thanks to you are doubly deep.

'As for the letter itself, I have understood it as follows:

'In wartime I am not merely permitted, but enjoined to kill every Arab man and woman whom I chance upon, if there is reason to fear that they help in the war against us, directly or indirectly. And as far as I am concerned I have to kill them even if that might result in an involvement with the military law. I think that this matter of the purity of weapons should be transmitted to educational institutions, at least the religious ones, so that they should have a position about this subject and so that they will not wander in the broad fields of "logic", especially on this subject; and the rule has to be explained as it should be followed in practice. For, I am sorry to say, I have seen different types of "logic" here even among the religious comrades. I do hope that you shall be active in this, so that our boys will know the line of their ancestors clearly and unambiguously.

'I conclude here, hoping that when the [training] course ends, in about a month, I shall be able to come to the yeshivah [talmudic college]. Greetings – *Moshe*.'

Of course, this doctrine of the Halakhah on murder clashes, in principle, not only with Israel's criminal law but also – as hinted in the letters just quoted – with official military standing regulations. However, there can be little doubt that in practice this doctrine does exert an influence on the administration of justice, especially by military authorities. The fact is that in all cases where Jews have, in a military or paramilitary context, murdered Arab non-combatants – including cases of mass murder such as that in Kafr Qasim in 1956 – the murderers, if not let off altogether, received extremely light sentences or won far-reaching remissions, reducing their punishment to next to nothing.[13]

Saving of Life

This subject – the supreme value of human life and the obligation of every human being to do the outmost to save the life of a fellow human – is of obvious importance in itself. It is also of particular interest in a Jewish context, in view of the fact that since the second world war Jewish opinion has – in some cases justly, in others unjustly – condemned 'the whole world' or at least all Europe for standing by when Jews were being massacred. Let us therefore examine what the Halakhah has to say on this subject.

According to the Halakhah, the duty to save the life of a fellow Jew is paramount.[14] It supersedes all other religious obligations and interdictions, excepting only the prohibitions against the three most heinous sins of adultery (including incest), murder and idolatry.

As for Gentiles, the basic talmudic principle is that their lives *must not* be saved, although it is also forbidden to murder them outright. The Talmud itself[15] expresses this in the maxim 'Gentiles are neither to be lifted [out of a well] nor hauled down [into it]'. Maimonides[16] explains:

> As for Gentiles with whom we are not at war ... their death must not be caused, but it is forbidden to save them if they are at the point of death; if, for example, one of them is seen falling into the sea, he should not be rescued, for it is written: 'neither shalt thou stand against the blood of thy fellow'[17] – but [a Gentile] is not thy fellow.

In particular, a Jewish doctor must not treat a Gentile patient. Maimonides – himself an illustrious physician – is quite explicit on this; in another passage[18] he repeats the distinction between 'thy fellow' and a Gentile, and concludes: 'and from this learn ye, that it is forbidden to heal a Gentile even for payment ... '

However, the refusal of a Jew – particularly a Jewish doctor – to save the life of a Gentile may, if it becomes known, antagonise powerful Gentiles and so put *Jews* in danger. Where such danger exists, the obligation to avert it supersedes the ban on helping the Gentile. Thus Maimonides continues: ' ... but if you fear him or his hostility, cure him for payment, though you are forbidden to do so without payment.' In fact, Maimonides himself was Saladin's personal physician. His insistence on demanding payment – presumably in order to make sure that the act is not one of human charity but an unavoidable duty – is however not absolute. For in another passage he allows Gentile whose hostility is feared to be treated 'even gratis, if it is unavoidable'.

The whole doctrine – the ban on saving a Gentile's life or healing him, and the suspension of this ban in cases where there is fear of hostility – is repeated (virtually verbatim) by other major authorities, including the 14th century *Arba'ah Turim* and Karo's *Beyt Yosef* and *Shulhan 'Arukh*.[19] *Beyt Yosef* adds, quoting Maimonides: 'And it is permissible to try out a drug on a heathen, if this serves a purpose'; and this is repeated also by the famous R. Moses Isserles.

The consensus of halakhic authorities is that the term 'Gentiles' in the above doctrine refers to *all* non-Jews. A lone voice of dissent is that of R. Moses Rivkes, author of a minor commentary on the *Shulhan 'Arukh*, who writes.[20]

> Our sages only said this about heathens, who in their day worshipped idols and did not believe in the Jewish Exodus from Egypt or in the creation of the world *ex nihilo*. But the Gentiles in whose [protective] shade we, the people of Israel, are exiled and among whom we are scattered do believe in the creation of the world *ex nihilo* and in the Exodus and in several principles of our own religion and they pray to the Creator of heaven and earth ... Not only is there no interdiction against helping them, but we are even obliged to pray for their safety.

This passage, dating from the second half of the 17th century, is a favourite quote of apologetic scholars.[21] Actually, it does not go nearly as far as the apologetics pretend, for it advocates *removing the ban* on saving a Gentile's life, rather than making it *mandatory* as in the case of a Jew; and even this liberality extends only to Christians and Muslims but not the majority of human beings. Rather, what it does show is that there was a way in which the harsh doctrine of the Halakhah *could have been* progressively liberalised. But as a matter of fact the majority of later halakhic authorities, far from extending Rivkes' leniency to other human groups, have rejected it altogether.

Desecrating the Sabbath to Save Life

Desecrating the sabbath – that is, doing work that would otherwise be banned on Saturday – becomes a duty when the need to save a Jew's life demands it.

The problem of saving a Gentile's life on the sabbath is not raised in the Talmud as a main issue, since it is in any case forbidden even on a weekday; it does however enter as a complicating factor in two connections.

First, there is a problem where a group of people are in danger, and it is possible (but not certain) that there is at least one Jew among them; should the sabbath be desecrated in order to save them? There is an extensive discussion of such cases. Following earlier authorities, including Maimonides and the Talmud itself, the *Shulhan 'Arukh*[22] decides these matters according to the weight of probabilities. For example, suppose nine Gentiles and one Jew live in the same building. One Saturday the building collapses; one of the ten – it is not known which one – is away, but the other nine are trapped under the rubble. Should the rubble be cleared, thus desecrating the sabbath, seeing that the Jew may not be under it (he may have been the one that got away)? The *Shulhan 'Arukh* says that it should, presumably because the odds that the Jew is under the rubble are high (nine to one). But now suppose that nine have got away and only one – again, it is not known which one – is trapped. Then there is no duty to clear the rubble, presumably because this time there are long odds (nine to one) *against* the Jew being the person trapped. Similarly: 'If a boat containing some Jews is seen to be in peril upon the sea, it is a duty incumbent upon all to desecrate the sabbath in order to save it.' However, the great R. 'Aqiva Eiger (died 1837) comments that this applies only 'when it is known that there are Jews on board. But ... if nothing at all is known about the identity of those on board, [the sabbath] must not be desecrated, for one acts according to [the weight of probabilities, and] the majority of people in the world are Gentiles.'[23] Thus, since there are very long odds against any of the passengers being Jewish, they must be allowed to drown.

Secondly, the provision that a Gentile may be saved or cared for in order to avert the danger of hostility is curtailed on the sabbath. A Jew called upon to help a Gentile on a weekday may have to comply because to admit that he is not allowed, in principle, to save the life of a non-Jew would be to invite hostility. But on Saturday the Jew can use sabbath observance as a plausible excuse. A paradigmatic case discussed at length in the Talmud[24] is that of a Jewish midwife invited to help a Gentile woman in childbirth. The upshot is that the midwife is allowed to help on a weekday 'for fear of hostility', but on the sabbath she must not do so, because she can excuse herself by saying: 'We are allowed to desecrate the sabbath only for our own, who observe the sabbath, but for your people, who do not keep the sabbath, we are not allowed to desecrate it.' Is this explanation a genuine one or merely an excuse? Maimonides clearly thinks that it is just an excuse, which can be used even if the task that the midwife is invited to do does not actually involve any desecration of the sabbath. Presumably, the excuse will work just as well even in this case, because Gentiles are generally in the dark as to precisely which kinds of work are banned for Jews on the sabbath. At any rate, he decrees: 'A Gentile woman must not be helped in childbirth on the sabbath, even for payment; nor must one fear hostility, even when [such help involves] no desecration of the sabbath.' The *Shulhan 'Arukh* decrees likewise.[25]

Nevertheless, this sort of excuse could not always be relied upon to do the trick and avert Gentile hostility. Therefore certain important rabbinical authorities had to relax the rules to some extent and allowed Jewish doctors to treat Gentiles on the sabbath even if this involved doing certain types of work normally banned on that day. This partial relaxation applied particularly to rich and powerful Gentile patients, who could not be fobbed off so easily and whose hostility could be dangerous.

Thus, R. Yo'el Sirkis, author of *Bayit Hadash* and one of the greatest rabbis of his time (Poland, 17th century), decided that 'mayors, petty nobles and aristocrats' should be treated on the sabbath, because of the fear of their hostility which involves 'some danger'. But in other cases, especially when the Gentile can be fobbed off with an evasive excuse, a Jewish doctor would commit 'an unbearable sin' by treating him on the sabbath. Later in the same century, a similar verdict was given in the French city of Metz, whose two parts were connected by a pontoon bridge. Jews are not normally allowed to cross such a bridge on the sabbath, but the rabbi of Metz decided that a Jewish doctor may nevertheless do so 'if he is called to the great governor': since the doctor is known to cross the bridge for the sake of his Jewish patients, the governor's hostility could be aroused if the doctor refused to do so for his sake. Under the authoritarian rule of Louis XIV, it was evidently important to have the goodwill of his intendant; the feelings of lesser Gentiles were of little importance.[26]

Hokhmat Shlomoh, a 19th century commentary on the *Shulhan 'Arukh*, mentions a similarly strict interpretation of the concept 'hostility' in connection with the Karaites, a small heretical Jewish sect. According to this view, their lives must not be saved if that would involve desecration of the sabbath, 'for "hostility" applies only to the heathen, who are many against us, and we are delivered into their hands .. But the Karaites are few and we are not delivered into their hands, [so] the fear of hostility does not apply to them at all.'[27] In fact, the *absolute* ban on desecrating the sabbath in order to save the life of a Karaite is still in force today, as we shall see.

The whole subject is extensively discussed in the *responsa* of R. Moshe Sofer - better known as 'Hatam Sofer' - the famous rabbi of Pressburg (Bratislava) who died in 1832. His conclusions are of more than historical interest, since in 1966 one of his *responsa* was publicly endorsed by the then Chief Rabbi of Israel as 'a basic institution of the Halakhah'.[28] The particular question asked of Hatam Sofer concerned the situation in Turkey, where it was decreed during one of the wars that in each township or village there should be midwives on call, ready to hire themselves out to any woman in labour. Some of these midwives were Jewish; should they hire themselves out to help Gentile women on weekdays and on the sabbath?

In his *responsum*,[29] Hatam Sofer first concludes, after careful investigation, that the Gentiles concerned – that is, Ottoman Christians and Muslims – are not only idolators 'who definitely worship other gods and thus should "neither be lifted [out of a well] nor hauled down",' but are likened by him to the Amalekites, so that the talmudic ruling 'it is forbidden to multiply the seed of Amalek' applies to them. In principle, therefore, they should not be helped even on weekdays. However, in practice it is 'permitted' to heal Gentiles and help them in labour, if they have doctors and midwives of their own, who could be called instead of the Jewish ones. For if Jewish doctors and midwives refused to attend to Gentiles, the only result would be loss of income to the former – which is of course undesirable. This applies equally on weekdays and on the sabbath, provided no desecration of the sabbath is involved. However, in the latter case the sabbath can serve as an excuse to 'mislead the heathen woman and say that it would involve desecration of the sabbath'.

In connection with cases that do actually involve desecration of the sabbath, Hatam Sofer – like other authorities – makes a distinction between two categories of work banned on the sabbath. First, there is work banned by the Torah, the biblical text (as interpreted by the Talmud); such work may only be performed in very exceptional cases, if failing to do so would cause an *extreme* danger of hostility towards Jews. Then there are types of work which are only banned by the sages who extended the original law of the Torah; the attitude towards breaking such bans is generally more lenient.

Another *responsum* of Hatam Sofer[30] deals with the question whether it is permissible for a Jewish doctor to travel by carriage on the sabbath in order to heal a Gentile. After pointing out that under certain conditions travelling by horse-drawn carriage on the sabbath only violates a ban imposed 'by the sages' rather than by the Torah, he goes on to recall

Maimonides' pronouncement that Gentile women in labour must not be helped on the sabbath, even if no desecration of the sabbath is involved, and states that the same principle applies to all medical practice, not just midwifery. But he then voices the fear that if this were put into practice, 'it would arouse undesirable hostility,' for 'the Gentiles would not accept the excuse of sabbath observance,' and 'would say that the blood of an idolator has little worth in our eyes'. Also, perhaps more importantly, Gentile doctors might take revenge on their Jewish patients. Better excuses must be found. He advises a Jewish doctor who is called to treat a Gentile patient out of town on the sabbath to excuse himself by saying that he is required to stay in town in order to look after his other patients, 'for he can use this in order to say, "I cannot move because of the danger to this or that patient, who needs a doctor first, and I may not desert my charge" ... With such an excuse there is no fear of danger, for it is a reasonable pretext, commonly given by doctors who are late in arriving because another patient needed them first.' Only 'if it is impossible to give any excuse' is the doctor permitted to travel by carriage on the sabbath in order to treat a Gentile.

In the whole discussion, the main issue is the excuses that should be made, not the actual healing or the welfare of the patient. And throughout it is taken for granted that it is all right to deceive Gentiles rather than treat them, so long as 'hostility' can be averted.[31]

Of course, in modern times most Jewish doctors are not religious and do not even know of these rules. Moreover, it appears that even many who are religious prefer – to their credit – to abide by the Hippocratic oath rather than by the precepts of their fanatic rabbis.[32] However, the rabbis' guidance cannot fail to have some influence on some doctors; and there are certainly many who, while not actually following that guidance, choose not to protest against it publicly.

All this is far from being a dead issue. The most up-to-date halakhic position on these matters is contained in a recent concise and authoritative book published in English under the title *Jewish Medical Law*.[33] This book, which bears the imprint of the prestigeous Israeli foundation *Mossad Harav Kook*, is based on the *responsa* of R. Eli'ezer Yehuda Waldenberg, Chief Justice of the Rabbinical District Court of Jerusalem. A few passages of this work deserve special mention.

First, 'it is forbidden to desecrate the sabbath ... for a Karaite.'[34] This is stated bluntly, absolutely and without any further qualification. Presumably the hostility of this small sect makes no difference, so they should be allowed to die rather than be treated on the sabbath.

As for Gentiles: 'According to the ruling stated in the Talmud and Codes of Jewish Law, it is forbidden to desecrate the Sabbath – whether violating Biblical or rabbinic law – in order to save the life of a dangerously ill gentile patient. It is also forbidden to deliver the baby of a gentile women on the Sabbath.'[35]

But this is qualified by a dispensation: 'However, today it is permitted to desecrate the Sabbath on behalf of a Gentile by performing actions prohibited by rabbinic law, for by so doing one prevents ill feelings from arising between Jew and Gentile.'[36]

This does not go very far, because medical treatment very often involves acts banned on the sabbath by the Torah itself, which are not covered by this dispensation. There are, we are told, 'some' halakhic authorities who extend the dispensation to such acts as well – but this is just another way of saying that *most* halakhic authorities, and the ones that really count, take the opposite view. However, all is not lost. *Jewish Medical Law* has a truly breathtaking solution to this difficulty.

The solution hangs upon a nice point of talmudic law. A ban imposed by the Torah on performing a given act on the sabbath is presumed to apply only when the primary intention in performing it is the actual outcome of the act. (For example, grinding wheat is presumed to be banned by the Torah only if the purpose is actually to obtain flour.) On the other hand, if the performance of the same act is merely incidental to some other purpose (*melakhah seh'eynah tzrikhah legufah*) then the act changes its status – it is still forbidden, to be sure, but only by the sages rather than by the Torah itself. Therefore:

> In order to avoid any transgression of the law, there is a legally acceptable method of rendering treatment on behalf of a gentile patient even when dealing with violation of Biblical Law. *It is suggested that at the time that the physician is providing the necessary care, his intentions should not primarily be to cure the patient, but to protect himself and the Jewish people from accusations of religious discrimination and severe retaliation that may endanger him in particular and the Jewish people in general.* With this intention, any act on the physician's part becomes 'an act whose actual outcome is not its primary purpose' ... which is forbidden on Sabbath only by rabbinic law.[37]

This hypocritical substitute for the Hippocratic oath is also proposed by a recent authoritative Hebrew book.[38]

Although the facts were mentioned at least twice in the

Israeli press,[39] the Israeli Medical Association has remained silent.

Having treated in some detail the supremely important subject of the attitude of the Halakhah to a Gentile's very life, we shall deal much more briefly with other halakhic rules which discriminate against Gentiles. Since the number of such rules is very large, we shall mention only the more important ones.

Sexual Offences

Sexual intercourse between a married Jewish woman and any man other than her husband is a capital offence for both parties, and one of the three most heinous sins. The status of Gentile women is very different. The Halakhah presumes all Gentiles to be utterly promiscuous and the verse 'whose flesh is as the flesh of asses, and whose issue [of semen] is like the issue of horses'[40] is applied to them. Whether a Gentile woman is married or not makes no difference, since as far as Jews are concerned the very concept of matrimony does not apply to Gentiles ('There is no matrimony for a heathen'). Therefore, the concept of adultery also does not apply to intercourse between a Jewish man and a Gentile woman; rather, the Talmud[41] equates such intercourse to the sin of bestiality. (For the same reason, Gentiles are generally presumed not to have certain paternity.)

According to the *Talmudic Encyclopedia*:[42] 'He who has carnal knowledge of the wife of a Gentile is not liable to the death penalty, for it is written: "thy fellow's wife"[43] rather than the alien's wife; and even the precept that a man "shall cleave unto his wife"[44] which is addressed to the Gentiles does not apply to a Jew, just there is no matrimony for a heathen; and although a married Gentile woman is forbidden to the Gentiles, in any case a Jew is exempted.'

This does not imply that sexual intercourse between a Jewish man and a Gentile woman is permitted – quite the contrary. But the main punishment is inflicted on the Gentile woman; she must be executed, even if she was raped by the Jew: 'If a Jew has coitus with a Gentile woman, whether she be a child of three or an adult, whether married or unmarried, and even if he is a minor aged only nine years and one day – because he had wilful coitus with her, she must be killed, as is the case with a beast, because through her a Jew got into trouble.'[45] The Jew, however, must be flogged, and if he is a Kohen (member of the priestly tribe) he must receive double the number of lashes, because he has committed a double offence: a Kohen must not have intercourse with a prostitute, and all Gentile women are presumed to be prostitutes.[46]

Status

According to the Halakhah, Jews must not (if they can help it) allow a Gentile to be appointed to any position of authority, however small, over Jews. (The two stock examples are 'commander over ten soldiers in the Jewish army' and 'superintendent of an irrigation ditch'.) Significantly, this particular rule applies also to converts to Judaism and to their descendants (through the female line) for ten generations or 'so long as the descent is known'.

Gentiles are presumed to be congenital liars, and are disqualified from testifying in a rabbinical court. In this respect their position is, in theory, the same as that of Jewish women, slaves and minors; but in practice it is actually worse. A Jewish woman is nowadays admitted as a witness to certain matters of fact, when the rabbinical court 'believes' her; a Gentile – never.

A problem therefore arises when a rabbinical court needs to establish a fact for which there are only Gentile witnesses. An important example of this is in cases concerning widows: by Jewish religious law, a woman can be declared a widow – and hence free to re-marry – only if the death of her husband is proven with certainty by means of a witness who saw him die or identified his corpse. However, the rabbinical court will accept the hearsay evidence of a Jew who testifies to having heard the fact in question mentioned by a Gentile eyewitness, provided the court is satisfied that the latter was speaking casually ('goy mesiah lefi tummo') rather than in reply to a direct question; for a Gentile's direct answer to a Jew's direct question is presumed to be a lie.[47] If necessary, a Jew (preferably a rabbi) will actually undertake to chat up the Gentile eyewitness and, without asking a direct question, extract from him a casual statement of the fact at issue.

Money and Property

1 *Gifts*. The Talmud bluntly forbids giving a gift to a Gentile. However, classical rabbinical authorities bent this rule because it is customary among businessmen to give gifts to business contacts. It was therefore laid down that a Jew may give a gift to a Gentile *acquaintance*, since this is regarded not as a true gift but as a sort of investment, for which some return is expected. Gifts to 'unfamiliar Gentiles' remain forbidden. A broadly similar rule applies to almsgiving. Giving alms to a Jewish beggar is an

important religious duty. Alms to Gentile beggars are merely permitted for the sake of peace. However there are numerous rabbinical warnings against allowing the Gentile poor to become 'accustomed' to receiving alms from Jews, so that it should be possible to withhold such alms without arousing undue hostility.

2 *Taking of interest.* Anti-Gentile discrimination in this matter has become largely theoretical, in view of the dispensation (explained in Chapter 3) which in effect allows interest to be exacted even from a Jewish borrower. However, it is still the case that granting an interest-free loan to a Jew is recommended as an act of charity, but from a Gentile borrower it is mandatory to exact interest. In fact, many – though not all – rabbinical authorities, including Maimonides, consider it mandatory to exact as much usury as possible on a loan to a Gentile.

3 *Lost property.* If a Jew finds property whose probable owner is Jewish, the finder is strictly enjoined to make a positive effort to return his find by advertising it publicly. In contrast, the Talmud and all the early rabbinical authorities not only allow a Jewish finder to appropriate an article lost by a Gentile, but actually forbid him or her to return it.[48] In more recent times, when laws were passed in most countries making it mandatory to return lost articles, the rabbinical authorities instructed Jews to do what these laws say, as an act of *civil* obedience to the state – but not as a religious duty, that is without making a positive effort to discover the owner if it is not probable that he is Jewish.

4 *Deception in business.* It is a grave sin to practice any kind of deception whatsoever against a Jew. Against a Gentile it is only forbidden to practice direct deception. Indirect deception is allowed, unless it is likely to cause hostility towards Jews or insult to the Jewish religion. The paradigmatic example is mistaken calculation of the price during purchase. If a Jew makes a mistake unfavourable to himself, it is one's religious duty to correct him. If a Gentile is spotted making such a mistake, one need not let him know about it, but say 'I rely on your calculation', so as to forestall his hostility in case he subsequently discovers his own mistake.

5 *Fraud.* It is forbidden to defraud a Jew by selling or buying at an unreasonable price. However, 'Fraud does not apply to Gentiles, for it is written: "Do not defraud each man his brother";[49] but a Gentile who defrauds a Jew should be compelled to make good the fraud, but should not be punished more severely than a Jew [in a similar case].'[50]

6 *Theft and robbery.* Stealing (without violence) is absolutely

forbidden – as the *Shulhan 'Arukh* so nicely puts it: 'even from a Gentile'. Robbery (with violence) is strictly forbidden if the victim is Jewish. However, robbery of a Gentile by a Jew is not forbidden outright but only under certain circumstances such as 'when the Gentiles are not under our rule', but is permitted 'when they are under our rule'. Rabbinical authorities differ among themselves as to the precise details of the circumstances under which a Jew may rob a Gentile, but the whole debate is concerned only with the relative power of Jews and Gentiles rather than with universal considerations of justice and humanity. This may explain why so very few rabbis have protested against the robbery of Palestinian property in Israel: it was backed by overwhelming Jewish power.

Gentiles in the Land of Israel

In addition to the general anti-Gentile laws, the Halakhah has special laws against Gentiles who live in the Land of Israel (*Eretz Yisra'el*) or, in some cases, merely pass through it. These laws are designed to promote Jewish supremacy in that country.

The exact geographical definition of the term 'Land of Israel' is much disputed in the Talmud and the talmudic literature, and the debate has continued in modern times between the various shades of zionist opinion. According to the maximalist view, the Land of Israel includes (in addition to Palestine itself) not only the whole of Sinai, Jordan, Syria and Lebanon, but also considerable parts of Turkey.[51] The more prevalent 'minimalist' interpretation puts the northern border 'only' about half way through Syria and Lebanon, at the latitude of Homs. This view was supported by Ben-Gurion. However, even those who thus exclude parts of Syria–Lebanon agree that certain special discriminatory laws (though less oppressive than in the Land of Israel proper) apply to the Gentiles of those parts, because that territory was included in David's kingdom. In all talmudic interpretations the Land of Israel includes Cyprus.

I shall now list a few of the special laws concerning Gentiles in the Land of Israel. Their connection with actual zionist practice will be quite apparent.

The Halakhah forbids Jews to sell immovable property – fields and houses – in the Land of Israel to Gentiles. In Syria, the sale of houses (but not of fields) is permitted.

Leasing a house in the Land of Israel to a Gentile is permitted under two conditions. First, that the house shall not be used for habitation but for other purposes, such as storage. Second, that three or more adjoining houses shall not be so leased.

These and several other rules are explained as follows: ... 'so that you shall not allow them to camp on the ground, for if they do not possess land, their sojourn there will be temporary.'52 Even temporary Gentile presence may only be tolerated 'when the Jews are in exile, or when the Gentiles are more powerful than the Jews,' but

> When the Jews are more powerful than the Gentiles we are forbidden to let an idolator among us; even a temporary resident or itinerant trader shall not be allowed to pass through our land unless he accepts the seven Noahide precepts,53 for it is written: 'they shall not dwell in thy land,'54 that is, not even temporarily. If he accepts the seven Noahide precepts, he becomes a resident alien (ger toshav) but it is forbidden to grant the status of resident alien except at times when the Jubilee is held [that is, when the Temple stands and sacrifices are offered]. However, during times when Jubilees are not held it is forbidden to accept anyone who is not a full convert to Judaism (ger tzedeq).55

It is therefore clear that – exactly as the leaders and sympathisers of Gush Emunim say – the whole question to how the Palestinians ought to be treated is, according to the Halakhah, simply a question of Jewish power: if Jews have sufficient power, then it is their religious duty to expel the Palestinians.

All these laws are often quoted by Israeli rabbis and their zealous followers. For example, the law forbidding the lease of three adjoining houses to Gentiles was solemnly quoted by a rabbinical conference held in 1979 to discuss the Camp David treaties. The conference also declared that according to the Halakhah even the 'autonomy' that Begin was ready to offer to the Palestinians is too liberal. Such pronouncements – which do in fact state correctly the position of the Halakhah – are rarely contested by the zionist 'left'.

In addition to laws such as those mentioned so far, which are directed at all Gentiles in the Land of Israel, an even greater evil influence arises from special laws against the ancient Canaanites and other nations who lived in Palestine before its conquest by Joshua, as well as against the Amalekites. All those nations must be utterly exterminated, and the Talmud and talmudic literature reiterate the genocidal biblical exhortations with even greater vehemence. Influential rabbis, who have a considerable following among Israeli army officers, identify the Palestinians (or even all Arabs) with those ancient nations, so that commands like 'thou shalt save alive nothing that breatheth'56 acquire a topical meaning. In fact, it is not uncommon for reserve soldiers called up to do a tour of duty in the Gaza Strip to be given an 'educational lecture' in which they are told that the Palestinians of Gaza are 'like the Amalekites'.

Biblical verses exhorting to genocide of the Midianites[57] were
solemnly quoted by an important Israeli rabbi in justification of
the Qibbiya massacre,[58] and this pronouncement has gained
wide circulation in the Israeli army. There are many similar
examples of bloodthirsty rabbinical pronouncements against the
Palestinians, based on these laws.

Abuse

Under this heading I would like to discuss examples of halakhic
laws whose most important effect is not so much to prescribe
specific anti-Gentile discrimination as to inculcate an attitude of
scorn and hatred towards Gentiles. Accordingly, in this section I
shall not confine myself to quoting from the most authoritative
halakhic sources (as I have done so far) but include also less
fundamental works, which are however widely used in religious
instruction.

Let us begin with the text of some common prayers. In one
of the first sections of the daily morning payer, every devout
Jew blesses God for not making him a Gentile.[59] The conclud-
ing section of the daily prayer (which is also used in the most
solemn part of the service on New Year's day and on Yom
Kippur) opens with the statement: 'We must praise the Lord of
all ... for not making us like the nations of [all] lands ... for
they bow down to vanity and nothingness and pray to a god
that does not help.'[60] The last clause was censored out of the
prayer books, but in eastern Europe it was supplied orally, and
has now been restored into many Israeli-printed prayer books.
In the most important section of the weekday prayer – the
'eighteen blessings' – there is a special curse, originally directed
against Christians, Jewish converts to Christianity and other
Jewish heretics: 'And may the apostates[61] have no hope, and all
the Christians perish instantly'. This formula dates from the
end of the 1st century, when Christianity was still a small
persecuted sect. Some time before the 14th century it was
softened into: 'And may the apostates have no hope, and all
the heretics[62] perish instantly', and after additional pressure
into: 'And may the informers have no hope, and all the heretics
perish instantly'. After the establishment of Israel, the process
was reversed, and many newly printed prayer books reverted to
the second formula, which was also prescribed by many teach-
ers in religious Israeli schools. After 1967, several congregations
close to Gush Emunim have restored the first version (so far
only verbally, not in print) and now pray daily that the Christians 'may perish instantly'. This process of reversion happened
in the period when the Catholic Church (under Pope John

XXIII) removed from its Good Friday service a prayer which asked the Lord to have mercy on Jews, heretics etc. This prayer was thought by most Jewish leaders to be offensive and even antisemitic.

Apart from the fixed daily prayers, a devout Jew must utter special short blessings on various occasions, both good and bad (for example, while putting on a new piece of clothing, eating a seasonal fruit for the first time that year, seeing powerful lightning, hearing bad news, etc.) Some of these occasional prayers serve to inculcate hatred and scorn for all Gentiles. We have mentioned in Chapter 2 the rule according to which a pious Jew must utter curse when passing near a Gentile cemetery, whereas he must bless God when passing near a Jewish cemetery. A similar rule applies to the living; thus, when seeing a large Jewish population a devout Jew must praise God, while upon seeing a large Gentile population he must utter a curse. Nor are buildings exempt: the Talmud lays down[63] that a Jew who passes near an inhabited non-Jewish dwelling must ask God to destroy it, whereas if the building is in ruins he must thank the Lord of Vengeance. (Naturally, the rules are reversed for Jewish houses.) This rule was easy to keep for Jewish peasants who lived in their own villages or for small urban communities living in all-Jewish townships or quarters. Under the conditions of classical Judaism, however, it became impracticable and was therefore confined to churches and places of worship of other religions (except Islam).[64] In this connection, the rule was further embroidered by custom: it became customary to spit (usually three times) upon seeing a church or a crucifix, as an embellishment to the obligatory formula of regret.[65] Sometimes insulting biblical verses were also added.[66]

There is also a series of rules forbidding any expression of praise for Gentiles or for their deeds, except where such praise implies an even greater praise of Jews and things Jewish. This rule is still observed by Orthodox Jews. For example, the writer Agnon, when interviewed on the Israeli radio upon his return from Stockholm, where he received the Nobel Prize for literature, praised the Swedish Academy, but hastened to add: 'I am not forgetting that it is forbidden to praise Gentiles, but here there is a special reason for my praise' – that is, that they awarded the prize to a Jew.

Similarly, it is forbidden to join any manifestation of popular Gentile rejoicing, except where failing to join in might cause 'hostility' towards Jews, in which case a 'minimal' show of joy is allowed.

In addition to the rules mentioned so far, there are many others whose effect is to inhibit human friendship between

Jew and Gentile. I shall mention two examples: the rule on 'libation wine' and that on preparing food for a Gentile on Jewish holy days.

A religious Jew must not drink any wine in whose preparation a Gentile had any part whatsoever. Wine in an open bottle, even if prepared wholly by Jews, becomes banned if a Gentile so much as touches the bottle or passes a hand over it. The reason given by the rabbis is that all Gentiles are not only idolators but must be presumed to be malicious to boot, so that they are likely to dedicate (by a whisper, gesture or thought) as 'libation' to their idol any wine which a Jew is about to drink. This law applies in full force to all Christians, and in a slightly attenuated form also to Muslims. (An open bottle of wine touched by a Christian must be poured away, but if touched by a Muslim it can be sold or given away, although it may not be drunk by a Jew.) The law applies equally to Gentile atheists (how can one be sure that they are not merely pretending to be atheists?) but not to Jewish atheists.

The laws against doing work on the sabbath apply to a lesser extent on other holy days. In particular, on a holy day which does not happen to fall on a Saturday it is permitted to do any work required for preparing food to be eaten during the holy days or days. Legally, this is defined as preparing a 'soul's food' (okhel nefesh); but 'soul' is interpreted to mean 'Jew', and 'Gentiles and dogs' are explicitly excluded.[67] There is, however, a dispensation in favour of powerful Gentiles, whose hostility can be dangerous: it is permitted to cook food on a holy day for a visitor belonging to this category, provided he is not actively encouraged to come and eat.

An important effect of all these laws – quite apart from their application in practice – is in the attitude created by their constant study which, as part of the study of the Halakhah, is regarded by classical Judaism as a supreme religious duty. Thus an Orthodox Jew learns from his earliest youth, as part of his sacred studies, that Gentiles are compared to dogs, that it is a sin to praise them, and so on and so forth. As a matter of fact, in this respect textbooks for beginners have a worse effect than the Talmud and the great talmudic codes. One reason for this is that such elementary texts give more detailed explanations, phrased so as to influence young and uneducated minds. Out of a large number of such texts, I have chosen the one which is currently most popular in Israel and has been reprinted in many cheap editions, heavily subsidised by the Israeli government. It is *The Book of Education*, written by an anonymous rabbi in early 14th century Spain. It explains the 613 religious obligations (*mitzvot*) of Judaism in the order in which they are supposed to be found in the Pentateuch according to the talmudic interpretation (discussed in Chapter 3). It owes its lasting influence and popularity to the clear and easy Hebrew style in which it is written.

A central didactic aim of this book is to emphasise the 'correct' meaning of the Bible with respect to such terms as 'fellow', 'friend' or 'man' (which we have referred to in Chapter 3). Thus §219, devoted to the religious obligation arising from the verse 'thou shalt love thy fellow as thyself', is entitled: 'A religious obligation to love Jews', and explains:

> To love every Jew strongly means that we should care for a Jew and his money just as one cares for oneself and one's own money, for it is written: 'thou shalt love thy fellow as thyself' and our sages of blessed memory said: 'what is hateful to you do not do to your friend' ... and many other religious obligations follow from this, because one who loves one's friend as oneself will not steal his money, or commit adultery with his wife, or defraud him of his money, or deceive him verbally, or steal his land, or harm him in any way. Also many other religious obligations depend on this, as is known to any reasonable man.

In §322, dealing with the *duty* to keep a Gentile slave enslaved for ever (whereas a Jewish slave must be set free after seven years), the following explanation is given:

> And at the root of this religious obligation [is the fact that] the Jewish people are the best of the human species, created to know their Creator and worship Him, and worthy of having slaves to serve them. And if they will not have slaves of other peoples, they would have to enslave their brothers, who would thus be unable to serve the Lord, blessed be He. Therefore we are commanded to possess those for our service, after they are prepared for this and after idolatory is removed from their speech so that there should not be danger in our houses,[68] and this is the intention of the verse 'but over your brethren the children of Israel, ye shall not rule one over another with rigour',[69] so that you will not have to enslave your brothers, who are all ready to worship God.

In §545, dealing with the religious obligation to exact interest on money lent to Gentiles, the law is stated as follows: 'That we are commanded to demand interest from Gentiles when we lend money to them, and we must not lend to them without interest,' The explanation is:

> And at the root of this religious obligation is that we should not do any act of mercy except to the people who know God and worship Him; and when we refrain from doing merciful

deed to the rest of mankind and do so only to the former, we are being tested that the main part of love and mercy to them is because they follow the religion of God, blessed be He. Behold, with this intention our reward [from God] when we withhold mercy from the others is equal to that for doing [merciful deeds] to members of our own people.

Similar distinctions are made in numerous other passages. In explaining the ban against delaying a worker's wage (§238) the author is careful to point out that the sin is less serious if the worker is Gentile. The prohibition against cursing (§239) is entitled 'Not to curse any Jew, whether man or woman'. Similarly, the prohibitions against giving misleading advice, hating other people, shaming them or taking revenge on them (§§240, 245, 246, 247) apply only to fellow-Jews.

The ban against following Gentile customs (§262) means that Jews must not only 'remove themselves' from Gentiles, but also 'speak ill of all their behaviour, even of their dress'.

It must be emphasised that the explanations quoted above do represent correctly the teaching of the Halakhah. The rabbis and, even worse, the apologetic 'scholars of Judaism' know this very well and for this reason they do not try to argue against such views inside the Jewish community; and of course they never mention them outside it. Instead, they vilify any Jew who raises these matters within earshot of Gentiles, and they issue deceitful denials in which the art of equivocation reaches its summit. For example, they state, using general terms, the importance which Judaism attaches to mercy; but what they forget to point out is that according to the Halakhah 'mercy' means mercy towards Jews.

Anyone who lives in Israel knows how deep and widespread these attitudes of hatred and cruelty to towards all Gentiles are among the majority of Israeli Jews. Normally these attitudes are disguised from the outside world, but since the establishment of the State of Israel, the 1967 war and the rise of Begin, a significant minority of Jews, both in Israel and abroad, have gradually become more open about such matters. In recent years the inhuman precepts according to which servitude is the 'natural' lot of Gentiles have been publicly quoted in Israel, even on TV, by Jewish farmers exploiting Arab labour, particularly child labour. Gush Emunim leaders have quoted religious precepts which enjoin Jews to oppress Gentiles, as a justification of the attempted assassination of Palestinian mayors and as divine authority for their own plan to expel all the Arabs from Palestine.

While many zionists reject these positions politically, their standard counter-arguments are based on considerations of expediency and Jewish self-interest, rather than on universally valid principles of humanism and ethics. For example, they argue that the exploitation and oppression of Palestinians by Israelis tends to corrupt Israeli society, or that the expulsion of the Palestinians is impracticable under present political conditions, or that Israeli acts of terror against the Palestinians tend to isolate Israel internationally. In principle, however, virtually all zionists – and in particular 'left' zionists – share the deep anti-Gentile attitudes which Orthodox Judaism keenly promotes.

Attitudes to Christianity and Islam

In the foregoing, several examples of the rabbinical attitudes to these two religions were given in passing. But it will be useful to summarise these attitudes here.

Judaism is imbued with a very deep hatred towards Christianity, combined with ignorance about it. This attitude was clearly aggravated by the Christian persecutions of Jews, but is largely independent of them. In fact, it dates from the time when Christianity was still weak and persecuted (not least by Jews), and it was shared by Jews who had never been persecuted by Christians or who were even helped by them. Thus, Maimonides was subjected to Muslim persecutions by the regime of the Almohads and escaped from them first to the crusaders' Kingdom of Jerusalem, but this did not change his views in the least. This deeply negative attitude is based on two main elements.

First, on hatred and malicious slanders against Jesus. The traditional view of Judaism on Jesus must of course be sharply distinguished from the nonsensical controversy between antisemites and Jewish apologists concerning the 'responsibility' for his execution. Most modern scholars of that period admit that due to the lack of original and contemporary accounts, the late composition of the Gospels and the contradictions between them, accurate historical knowledge of the circumstances of Jesus' execution is not available. In any case, the notion of collective and inherited guilt is both wicked and absurd. However, what is at issue here is not the actual facts about Jesus, but the inaccurate and even slanderous reports in the Talmud and post-talmudic literature – which is what Jews believed until the 19th century and many, especially in Israel, still believe. For these reports certainly played an important role in forming the Jewish attitude to Christianity.

According to the Talmud, Jesus was executed by a proper rabbinical court for idolatry, inciting other Jews to idolatry, and contempt of rabbinical authority. All classical Jewish sources which mention his execution are quite happy to take responsibility for it; in the talmudic account the Romans are not even mentioned.

The more popular accounts – which were nevertheless taken quite seriously – such as the notorious *Toldot Yeshu* are even worse, for in addition to the above crimes they accuse him of witchcraft. The very name 'Jesus' was for Jews a symbol of all that is abominable, and this popular tradition still persists.[70] The Gospels are equally detested, and they are not allowed to be quoted (let alone taught) even in modern Israeli Jewish schools.

Secondly, for theological reasons, mostly rooted in ignorance, Christianity as a religion is classed by rabbinical teaching as idolatry. This is based on a crude interpretation of the Christian doctrines on the Trinity and Incarnation. All the Christian emblems and pictorial representations are regarded as 'idols' – even by those Jews who literally worship scrolls, stones or personal belongings of 'Holy Men'.

The attitude of Judaism towards Islam is, in contrast, relatively mild. Although the stock epithet given to Muhammad is 'madman' (*'meshugga'*), this was not nearly as offensive as it may sound now, and in any case it pales before the abusive terms applied to Jesus. Similarly, the Qur'an – unlike the New Testament – is not condemned to burning. It is not honoured in the same way as Islamic law honours the Jewish sacred scrolls, but is treated as an ordinary book. Most rabbinical authorities agree that Islam is *not* idolatry (although some leaders of Gush Emunim now choose to ignore this). Therefore the Halakhah decrees that Muslims should not be treated by Jews any worse than 'ordinary' Gentiles. But also no better. Again, Maimonides can serve as an illustration. He explicitly states that Islam is not idolatry, and in his philosophical works he quotes, with great respect, many Islamic philosophical authorities. He was, as I have mentioned before, personal physician to Saladin and his family, and by Saladin's order he was appointed Chief over all Egypt's Jews. Yet, the rules he lays down against saving a Gentile's life (except in order to avert danger to Jews) apply equally to Muslims.

Chapter 6

Political Consequences

The persistent attitudes of classical Judaism toward non-Jews strongly influence its followers, Orthodox Jews and those who can be regarded as its continuators, zionists. Through the latter it also influences the policies of the State of Israel. Since 1967, as Israel becomes more and more 'Jewish', so its policies are influenced more by Jewish ideological considerations than by those of a coldly conceived imperial interest. This ideological influence is not usually perceived by foreign experts, who tend to ignore or downplay the influence of the Jewish religion on Israeli policies. This explains why many of their predictions are incorrect.

In fact, more Israeli government crises are caused by religious reasons, often trivial, than by any other cause. The space devoted by the Hebrew press to discussion of the constantly occurring quarrels between the various religious groups, or between the religious and the secular, is greater than that given any other subject, except in times of war or of security-related tension. At the time of writing, early August 1993, some topics of major interest to readers of the Hebrew press are: whether soldiers killed in action who are sons of non-Jewish mothers will be buried in a segregated area in Israeli military cemeteries; whether Jewish religious burial associations, who have a monopoly over the burial of all Jews except kibbutz members, will be allowed to continue their custom of circumcising the corpses of non-circumcised Jews before burying them (and without asking the family's permission); whether the import of non-kosher meat to Israel, banned unofficially since the establishment of the state, will be allowed or banned by law. There are many more issues of this kind which are of a much greater interest to the Israeli-Jewish public than, let us say, the negotiations with the Palestinians and Syria.

The attempts made by a few Israeli politicians to ignore the factors of 'Jewish ideology' in favour of purely imperial interests have led to disastrous results. In early 1974, after its partial defeat in the Yom Kippur War, Israel had a vital interest in stopping the renewed influence of the PLO, which had not yet been recognised by the Arab states as the solely legitimate representative of the Palestinians. The Israeli government conceived of a plan to support Jordanian influence in the West Bank, which was quite considerable at the time. When King Hussein was asked for his support, he demanded a visible *quid pro quo*. It was arranged that his chief West Bank supporter, Sheikh Jabri of Hebron, who ruled the southern part of the West Bank with an iron fist and with approval of then Defence minister Moshe Dayan, would give a party for the region's notables in the courtyard of his palatial residence in Hebron. The party, in honour of the king's birthday, would feature the public display of Jordanian flags and would begin a pro-Jordanian campaign. But the religious settlers in the nearby Kiryat-Arba, who were only a handful at the time, heard about the plan and threatened Prime Minister Golda Meir and Dayan with vigorous protests since, as they put it, displaying a flag of a 'non-Jewish state' within the Land of Israel contradicts the sacred principle which states that this land 'belongs' only to Jews. Since this principle is accepted by all zionists, the government had to bow to their demands and order Sheikh Jabri not to display any Jordanian flags. Thereupon Jabri, who was deeply humiliated, cancelled the party and, at the Fez meeting of the Arab League which occurred soon after, King Hussein voted to recognise the PLO as the sole representative of the Palestinians. For the bulk of Israeli-Jewish public the current negotiations about 'autonomy' are likewise influenced more by such Jewish ideological considerations than by any others.

The conclusion from this consideration of Israeli policies, supported by an analysis of classical Judaism, must be that analyses of Israeli policy-making which do not emphasise the importance of its unique character as a 'Jewish state' must be mistaken. In particular, the facile comparison of Israel to other cases of Western imperialism or to settler states, is incorrect. During apartheid, the land of South Africa was officially divided into 87 per cent which 'belonged' to the whites and 13 per cent which was said officially to 'belong' to the Blacks. In addition, officially sovereign states, embodied with all the symbols of sovereignty, the so-called Bantustans, were established. But 'Jewish ideology' demands that no part of the Land of Israel can be recognised as 'belonging' to non-Jews and that no signs of sovereignty, such as Jordanian flags, can be officially allowed to be displayed. The principle of Redemption of the Land demands that ideally *all* the land, and not merely, say, 87 per cent, will in time be 'redeemed', that is, become owned by Jews. 'Jewish ideology prohibits that very convenient principle of imperialism, already known to Romans and followed by so many secular empires, and best formulated by Lord Cromer: 'We do not govern Egypt, we govern the governors of Egypt.'

Jewish ideology forbids such recognition; it also forbids a seemingly respectful attitude to any 'non-Jewish governors' within
the Land of Israel. The entire apparatus of client kings, sultans,
maharajas and chiefs or, in more modern times, of dependent
dictators, so convenient in other cases of imperial hegemony,
cannot be used by Israel within the area considered part of the
Land of Israel. Hence the fears, commonly expressed by Palestinians, of being offered a 'Bantustan' are totally groundless.
Only if numerous Jewish lives are lost in war, as happened
both in 1973 and in the 1983–5 war aftermath in Lebanon, is
an Israeli retreat conceivable since it can be justified by the
principle that the sanctity of Jewish life is more important than
other considerations. What is not possible, as long as Israel
remains a 'Jewish state', is the Israeli grant of a fake, but
nevertheless symbolically real sovereignty, or even of real autonomy, to non-Jews within the Land of Israel for merely
political reasons. Israel, like some other countries, is an exclusivist state, but Israeli exclusivism is peculiar to itself.

In addition to Israeli policies it may be surmised that the
'Jewish ideology' influences also a significant part, maybe a
majority, of the diaspora Jews. While the actual implementation
of Jewish ideology depends on Israel being strong, this in turn
depends to a considerable extent on the support which diaspora
Jews, particularly US Jews, give to Israel. The image of the
diaspora Jews and their attitudes to non-Jews, is quite different
from the attitudes of classical Judaism, as described above. This
discrepancy is most obvious in English-speaking countries,
where the greatest falsifications of Judaism regularly occur. The
situation is worst in the USA and Canada, the two states
whose support for Israeli policies, including policies which most
glaringly contradict the basic human rights of non-Jews, is
strongest.

US support for Israel, when considered not in abstract but
in concrete detail, cannot be adequately explained only as a
result of American imperial interests. The strong influence
wielded by the organised Jewish community in the USA in
support of all Israeli policies must also be taken into account
in order to explain the Middle East policies of American
administrations. This phenomenon is even more noticeable in
the case of Canada, whose Middle Eastern interests cannot
be considered as important, but whose loyal dedication to
Israel is even greater than that of the USA. In both countries (and also in France, Britain and many other states)
Jewish organisations support Israel with about the same loyalty which communist parties accorded to the USSR for so
long. Also, many Jews who appear to be active in defending

human rights and who adopt non-conformist views on other issues do, in cases affecting Israel, display a remarkable degree of totalitarianism and are in the forefront of the defence of all Israeli policies. It is well known in Israel that the chauvinism and fanaticism in supporting Israel displayed by organised diaspora Jews is much greater (especially since 1967) than the chauvinism shown by an average Israeli Jew. This fanaticism is especially marked in Canada and the USA but because of the incomparably greater political importance of the USA, I will concentrate on the latter. It should, however, be noted that we also find Jews whose views of Israeli policies are not different from those held by the rest of the society (with due regard to the factors of geography, income, social position and so on).

Why should some American Jews display chauvinism, sometimes extreme, and others not? We should begin by observing the social and therefore also the political importance of the Jewish organisations which are of an exclusive nature: they admit no non-Jews on principle. (This exclusivism is in amusing contrast with their hunt to condemn the most obscure non-Jewish club which refuses to admit Jews.) Those who can be called 'organised Jews', and who spend most of their time outside work hours mostly in the company of other Jews, can be presumed to uphold Jewish exclusivism and to preserve the attitudes of the classical Judaism to non-Jews. Under present circumstances they cannot openly express these attitudes toward non-Jews in the USA where non-Jews constitute more than 97 per cent of the population. They compensate for this by expressing their real attitudes in their support of the 'Jewish state' and the treatment it metes to the non-Jews of the Middle East.

How else can we explain the enthusiasm displayed by so many American rabbis in support of, let us say, Martin Luther King, compared with their lack of support for the rights of Palestinians, even for their individual human rights? How else can we explain the glaring contradiction between the attitudes of classical Judaism toward non-Jews, which include the rule that their lives should not be saved except for the sake of Jewish interest, with the support of the US rabbis and organised Jews for the rights of the Blacks? After all, Martin Luther King and the majority of American Blacks are non-Jews. Even if only the conservative and Orthodox Jews, who together constitute the majority of organised American Jews, are considered to hold such opinions about the non-Jews, the other part of organised US Jewry, the Reform, had never opposed them, and, in my view, show themselves to be quite influenced by them.

Actually the explanation of this apparent contradiction is easy. It should be recalled that Judaism, especially in its classical form, is totalitarian in nature. The behaviour of supporters of other totalitarian ideologies of our times was not different from that of the organised American Jews. Stalin and his supporters never tired of condemning the discrimination against the American or the South African Blacks, especially in the midst of the worst crimes committed within the USSR. The South African apartheid regime was tireless in its denunciations of the violations of human rights committed either by communist or by other African regimes, and so were its supporters in other countries. Many similar examples can be given. The support of democracy or of human rights is therefore meaningless or even harmful and deceitful when it does not begin with self-critique and with support of human rights when they are violated by one's own group. Any support of human rights in general by a Jew which does not include the support of human rights of non-Jews whose rights are being violated by the 'Jewish state' is as deceitful as the support of human rights by a Stalinist. The apparent enthusiasm displayed by American rabbis or by the Jewish organisations in the USA during the 1950s and the 1960s in support of the Blacks in the South, was motivated only by considerations of Jewish self-interest, just as was the communist support for the same Blacks. Its purpose in both cases was to try to capture the Black community politically, in the Jewish case to an unthinking support of Israeli policies in the Middle East.

Therefore, the real test facing both Israeli and diaspora Jews is the test of their self-criticism which must include the critique of the Jewish past. The most important part of such a critique must be detailed and honest confrontation of the Jewish attitude to non-Jews. This is what many Jews justly demand from non-Jews: to confront their own past and so become aware of the discrimination and persecutions inflicted on the Jews. In the last 40 years the number of non-Jews killed by Jews is by far greater than the number of the Jews killed by non-Jews. The extent of the persecution and discrimination against non-Jews inflicted by the 'Jewish state' with the support of organised diaspora Jews is also enormously greater than the suffering inflicted on Jews by regimes hostile to them. Although the struggle against antisemitism (and of all other forms of racism) should never cease, the struggle against Jewish chauvinism and exclusivism, which must include a critique of classical Judaism, is now of equal or greater importance.

Notes and References

Chapter 1: A Closed Utopia?

1 Walter Laquer, *History of Zionism*, Schocken Publishers, Tel Aviv, 1974, in Hebrew.

2 See Yedioth Ahronot, 27 April 1992.

3 In Hugh Trevor-Roper, *Renaissance Essays*, Fontana Press, London, 1985.

4 See Moses Hadas, *Hellenistic Culture, Fusion and Diffusion*, Columbia University Press, New York, 1959, especially chapters VII and XX.

Chapter 2: Prejudice and Prevarication

1 The Jews themselves universally described themselves as a religious community or, to be precise, a *religious nation*. 'Our people is a people only because of the *Torah* (Religious Law)' – this saying by one of the highest authorities, Rabbi Sa'adia Hagga'on who lived in the 10th century, has become proverbial.

2 By Emperor Joseph II in 1782.

3 All this is usually omitted in vulgar Jewish historiography, in order to propagate the myth that the Jews kept their religion by miracle or by some peculiar mystic force.

4 For example, in her *Origins of Totalitarianism*, a considerable part of which is devoted to Jews.

5 Before the end of the 18th century, German Jews were allowed by their rabbis to write German in Hebrew letters only, on pain of being excommunicated, flogged, etc.

6 When by a deal between the Roman Empire and the Jewish leaders (the dynasty of the *Nesi'im*) all the Jews in the Empire were subjected to the fiscal and disciplinary authority of these leaders and their rabbinical courts, who for their part undertook to keep order among the Jews.

7 I write this, being a non-socialist myself. But I will honour and respect people with whose principles I disagree, if they make an honest effort to be true to their principles. In contrast, there is nothing so despicable as the dishonest use of universal principles, whether true or false, for the selfish ends of an individual or, even worse, of a group.

8 In fact, many aspects of orthodox Judaism were apparently derived from Sparta, through the baneful political influence

of Plato. On this subject, see the excellent comments of Moses Hadas, *Hellenistic Culture, Fusion and Diffusion*, Columbia University Press, New York, 1959.

9 Including the geography of Palestine and indeed its very location. This is shown by the orientation of all synagogues in countries such as Poland and Russia: Jews are supposed to pray facing Jerusalem, and the European Jews, who had only a vague idea where Jerusalem was, always assumed it was due east, whereas for them it was in fact more nearly due south.

10 Throughout this chapter I use the term 'classical Judaism' to refer to rabbinical Judaism as it emerged after about AD 800 and lasted up to the end of the 18th century. I avoid the term 'normative Judaism', which many authors use with roughly the same meaning, because in my view it has unjustified connotations.

11 The works of Hellenistic Jews, such as Philo of Alexandria, constitute an exception. They were written before classical Judaism achieved a position of exclusive hegemony. They were indeed subsequently suppressed among the Jews and survived only because Christian monks found them congenial.

12 During the whole period from AD 100 to 1500 there were written two travel books and one history of talmudic studies – a short, inaccurate and dreary book, written moreover by a despised philosopher (Abraham ben-David, Spain, c. 1170).

13 *Me'or 'Eynayim* by 'Azarya de Rossi of Ferrara, Italy, 1574.

14 The best known cases were in Spain; for example (to use their adopted Christian names) Master Alfonso of Valladolid, converted in 1320, and Paul of Santa Maria, converted in 1390 and appointed bishop of Burgos in 1415. But many other cases can be cited from all over west Europe.

15 Certainly the tone, and also the consequences, were very much better than in disputations in which Christians were accused of heresy – for example those in which Peter Abelard or the strict Franciscans were condemned.

16 The stalinist and Chinese examples are sufficiently well known. However, it is worth mentioning that the persecution of honest historians in Germany began very early. In 1874, H. Ewald, a professor at Goettingen, was imprisoned for expressing 'incorrect' views on the conquests of Frederick II, a hundred years earlier. The situation in Israel is analogous: the worst attacks against me were provoked not by the violent terms I employ in my condemnations of zionism and the oppression of Palestinians, but by an early article of mine about the role of Jews in the slave trade, in which the latest case quoted dated from 1870. That article was published before the 1967 war; nowadays its publication would be impossible.

17   In the end a few other passages also had to be removed, such as those which seemed theologically absurd (for example, where God is said to pray to Himself or physically to carry out some of the practices enjoined on the individual Jew) or those which celebrated too freely the sexual escapades of ancient rabbis.

18   *Tractate Berakhot*, p. 58b.

19   'Your mother shall be sore confounded; she that bare you shall be ashamed ...', *Jeremiah*, 50:12.

20   Published by Boys Town, Jerusalem, and edited by Moses Hyamson, one of the most reputable scholars of Judaism in Britain.

21   The supposed founders of the Sadducean sect.

22   I am happy to say that in a recent new translation (Chicago University Press) the word 'Blacks' does appear, but the heavy and *very expensive* volume is unlikely, as yet, to get into the 'wrong' hands. Similarly, in early 19th century England, radical books (such as Godwin's) were allowed to appear, provided they were issued in a very expensive edition.

23   An additional fact can be mentioned in this connection. It was perfectly possible, and apparently respectable, for a Jewish scholar of Islam, Bernard Lewis (who formerly taught in London and is now teaching in the USA) to publish an article in *Encounter*, in which he points out many passages in Islamic literature which in his view are anti-Black, but none of which even approaches the passage quoted above. It would be quite impossible for anyone now, or in the last thirty years, to discuss in any reputable American publication the above passage or the many other offensive anti-Black talmudic passages. But without a criticism of *all* sides the attack on Islam alone reduces to mere slander.

Chapter 3: Orthodoxy and Interpretation

1   As in Chapter 2, I use the term 'classical Judaism' to refer to rabbinical Judaism in the period from about AD 800 up to the end of the 18th century. This period broadly coincides with the Jewish Middle Ages, since for most Jewish communities medieval conditions persisted much longer than for the west European nations, namely up to the period of the French Revolution. Thus what I call 'classical Judaism' can be regarded as *medieval* Judaism.

2   *Exodus*, 15:11.

3   Ibid., 20:3-6.

4   *Jeremiah*, 10; the same theme is echoed still later by the Second Isaiah, see *Isaiah*, 44.

5   The cabbala is of course an esoteric doctrine, and its de-
     tailed study was confined to scholars. In Europe, especially
     after about 1750, extreme measures were taken to keep it
     secret and forbid its study except by mature scholars and
     under strict supervision. The uneducated Jewish masses of
     eastern Europe had no real knowledge of cabbalistic doc-
     trine; but the cabbala percolated to them in the form of
     superstition and magic practices.

6   Many contemporary Jewish mystics believe that the same
     end may be accomplished more quickly by war against the
     Arabs, by the expulsion of the Palestinians, or even by
     establishing many Jewish settlements on the West Bank. The
     growing movement for building the Third Temple is also
     based on such ideas.

7   The Hebrew word used here – *yihud*, meaning literally union-
     in-seclusion – is the same one employed in legal texts (deal-
     ing with marriage etc.) to refer to sexual intercourse.

8   The so-called *Qedushah Shlishit* (Third Holiness), inserted in
     the prayer *Uva Letzion* towards the end of the morning
     service.

9   *Numbers*, 29.

10   The power of Satan, and his connection with non-Jews, is
     illustrated by a widespread custom, established under cabba-
     listic influence in many Jewish communities from the 17th
     century. A Jewish woman returning from her monthly ritual
     bath of purification (after which sexual intercourse with her
     husband is mandatory) must beware of meeting one of the
     four satanic creatures: Gentile, pig, dog or donkey. If she
     does meet any one of them she must take another bath. The
     custom was advocated (among others) by *Shevet Musar*, a
     book on Jewish moral conduct first published in 1712, which
     was one of the most popular books among Jews in both
     eastern Europe and Islamic countries until early this century,
     and is still widely read in some Orthodox circles.

11   This is prescribed in minute detail. For example, the ritual
     hand washing must not be done under a tap; each hand
     must be washed singly, in water from a mug (of prescribed
     minimal size) held in the other hand. If one's hands are
     really dirty, it is quite impossible to clean them in this way,
     but such pragmatic considerations are obviously irrelevant.
     Classical Judaism prescribes a great number of such detailed
     rituals, to which the cabbala attaches deep significance.
     There are, for example, many precise rules concerning be-
     haviour in a lavatory. A Jew relieving nature in an open
     space must not do so in a North–South direction, because
     North is associated with Satan.

12   'Interpretation' is my own expression. The classical (and
     present-day Orthodox) view is that the talmudic meaning,

even where it is contrary to the literal sense, was always the operational one.

13   According to an apocryphal story, a famous 19th century Jewish heretic observed in this connection that the verse 'Thou shalt not commit adultery' is repeated only twice. 'Presumably one is therefore forbidden to eat adultery or to cook it, but enjoying it is all right.'

14   The Hebrew *re'akha* is rendered by the King James Version (and most other English translations) somewhat imprecisely as 'thy neighbour'. See however *II Samuel*, 16:17, where exactly the same word is rendered by the King James Version more correctly as 'thy friend'.

15   The Mishnah is remarkably free of all this, and in particular the belief in demons and witchcraft is relatively rare in it. The Babylonian Talmud, on the other hand, is full of gross superstitions.

16   Or, to be precise, in many parts of Palestine. Apparently the areas to which the law applies are those where there was Jewish demographic predominance around AD 150–200.

17   Therefore non-zionist Orthodox Jews in Israel organise special shops during sabbatical years, which sell fruits and vegetables grown by Arabs on Arab land.

18   In the winter of 1945–6, I myself, then a boy under 13, participated in such proceedings. The man in charge of agricultural work in the religious agricultural school I was then attending was a particularly pious Jew and thought it would be safe if the crucial act, that of removing the board, should be performed by an orphan under 13 years old, incapable of being, or making anyone else, guilty of a sin. (A boy under that age cannot be guilty of a sin; his father, if he has one, is considered responsible.) Everything was carefully explained to me beforehand, including the duty to say, 'I need this board,' when in fact it was not needed.

19   For example, the Talmud forbids a Jew to enjoy the light of a candle lit by a Gentile on the sabbath, unless the latter had lit it for his own use before the Jew entered the room.

20   One of my uncles in pre-1939 Warsaw used a subtler method. He employed a non-Jewish maid called Marysia and it was his custom upon waking from his Saturday siesta to say, first quietly, 'How nice it would be if' – and then, raising his voice to a shout, '... Marysia would bring us a cup of tea!' He was held to be a very pious and God-fearing man and would never dream of drinking a drop of milk for a full six hours after eating meat. In his kitchen he had two sinks, one for washing up dishes used for eating meat, the other for milk dishes.

21   Occasionally regrettable mistakes occur, because some of these jobs are quite cushy, allowing the employee six days off

each week. The town of Bney Braq (near Tel-Aviv), inhabited almost exclusively by Orthodox Jews, was shaken in the 1960s by a horrible scandal. Upon the death of the 'sabbath-Goy' they had employed for over twenty years to watch over their water supplies on Saturdays, it was discovered that he was not really a Christian but a Jew! So when his successor, a Druse, was hired, the town demanded and obtained from the government a document certifying that the new employee is a Gentile of pure Gentile descent. It is reliably rumoured that the secret police was asked to research this matter.

22 In contrast, elementary Scripture teaching can be done for payment. This was always considered a low-status job and was badly paid.

23 Another 'extremely important' ritual is the blowing of a ram's horn on Rosh Hashanah, whose purpose is to confuse Satan.

Chapter 4: The Weight of History

1 See, for example, *Jeremiah*, 44, especially verses 15–19. For an excellent treatment of certain aspects of this subject see Raphael Patai, *The Hebrew Goddess*, Ktav, USA, 1967.

2 *Ezra*, 7:25–26. The last two chapters of this book are mainly concerned with Ezra's efforts to segregate the 'pure' Jews ('the holy seed') away from 'the people of the land' (who were themselves at least partly of Jewish descent) and break up mixed marriages.

3 W.F. Albright, *Recent Discoveries in Bible Lands*, Funk & Wagnall, New York, 1955, p. 103.

4 It is significant that, together with this literary corpus, *all* the historical books written by Jews after about 400 BC were also rejected. Until the 19th century, Jews were quite ignorant of the story of Massadah and of figures such as Judas Maccabaeus, now regarded by many (particularly by Christians) as belonging to the 'very essence' of Judaism.

5 *Acts*, 18:15.

6 Ibid., 25.

7 See note 6 to Chapter 2.

8 Concerning the term 'classical Judaism' see note 10 to Chapter 2 and note 1 to Chapter 3.

9 Nobel Prize winners Agnon and Bashevis Singer are examples of this, but many others can be given, particularly Bialik, the national Hebrew poet. In his famous poem *My Father* he describes his saintly father selling vodka to the drunkard peasants who are depicted as animals. This very popular poem, taught in all Israeli schools, is one of the vehicles through which the anti-peasant attitude is reproduced.

10 So far as the central power of the Jewish Patriarchate was

concerned, the deal was terminated by Theodosius II in a series of laws, culminating in AD 429; but many of the local arrangements remained in force.

11   Perhaps another characteristic example is the Parthian empire (until AD 225) but not enough is known about it. We know, however, that the establishment of the national Iranian Sasanid empire brought about an immediate decline of the Jews' position.

12   This ban extends also to marrying a woman converted to Judaism, because all Gentile women are presumed by the Halakhah to be prostitutes.

13   A prohibited marriage is not generally void, and requires a divorce. Divorce is nominally a voluntary act on the part of the husband, but under certain circumstances a rabbinical court can coerce him to 'will' it (kofin oto 'ad sheyyomar rotzeh ani).

14   Although Jewish achievements during the Golden Age in Muslim Spain (1002–1147) were more brilliant, they were not lasting. For example, most of the magnificent Hebrew poetry of that age was subsequently forgotten by Jews, and only recovered by them in the 19th or 20th century.

15   During that war, Henry of Trastamara used anti-Jewish propaganda, although his own mother, Leonor de Guzman, a high Castilian noblewoman, was partly of Jewish descent. (Only in Spain did the highest nobility intermarry with Jews.) After his victory he too employed Jews in the highest financial positions.

16   Until the 18th century the position of serfs in Poland was generally supposed to be even worse than in Russia. In that century, certain features of Russian serfdom, such as public sales of serfs, got worse than in Poland but the central Tsarist government always retained certain powers over the enslaved peasants, for example the right to recruit them to the national army.

17   During the preceding period persecutions of Jews were rare. This is true of the Roman Empire even after serious Jewish rebellions. Gibbon is correct in praising the liberality of Antoninus Pius (and Marcus Aurelius) to Jews, so soon after the major Bar-Kokhba rebellion of AD 132–5.

18   This fact, easily ascertainable by examination of the details of each persecution, is not remarked upon by most general historians in recent times. An honourable exception is Hugh Trevor-Roper, The Rise of Christian Europe, Thames and Hudson, London, 1965, pp. 173–4. Trevor-Roper is also one of the very few modern historians who mention the predominant Jewish role in the early medieval slave trade between Christian (and pagan) Europe and the Muslim world (ibid., pp. 92–3). In order to promote this abomination, which I

have no space to discuss here. Maimonides allowed Jews, in the name of the Jewish religion, to abduct Gentile children into slavery; and his opinion was no doubt acted upon or reflected contemporary practice.

19 Examples can be found in any history of the crusades. See especially S. Runciman, *A History of the Crusades*, vol I, book 3, chap 1, 'The German Crusade'. The subsequent defeat of this host by the Hungarian army, 'to most Christians appeared as a just punishment meted out of high to the murderers of the Jews.'

20 John Stoye, *Europe Unfolding 1648–88*, Fontana, London, p. 46.

21 This latter feature is of course not mentioned by received Jewish historiography. The usual punishment for a rebellious, or even 'impudent' peasant was impalement.

22 The same can be observed in different regions of a given country. For example, in Germany, agrarian Bavaria was much more antisemitic than the industrialised areas.

23 'The refusal of the Church to admit that once a Jew always a Jew, was another cause of pain for an ostentatious Catholic like Drumont. One of his chief lieutenants, Jules Guérin, has recounted the disgust he felt when the famous Jesuit, Père du Lac, remonstrated with him for attacking some converted Jews named Dreyfus.' D.W. Brogan, *The Development of Modern France*, vol 1, Harper Torchbooks, New York, 1966, p. 227.

24 Ibid.

25 Let me illustrate the irrational, demonic character which racism can sometimes acquire with three examples chosen at random. A major part of the extermination of Europe's Jews was carried out in 1942 and early 1943 during the Nazi offensive in Russia, which culminated in their defeat at Stalingrad. During the eight months between June 1942 and February 1943 the Nazis probably used more railway wagons to haul Jews to the gas chambers than to carry much needed supplies to the army. Before being taken to their death, most of these Jews, at least in Poland, had been very effectively employed in production of equipment for the German army. The second, rather remote, example comes from a description of the Sicilian Vespers in 1282: 'Every Frenchman they met was struck down. They poured into the inns frequented by the French and the houses where they dwelt, sparing neither man nor woman nor child ... The rioters broke into the Dominican and Franciscan convents, and all the foreign friars were dragged out and told to pronounce the word *ciciri*, whose sound the French tongue could never accurately reproduce. Anyone who failed in the test was slain.' (S. Runciman, *The Sicilian Vespers*, Cam-

bridge University Press, 1958, p. 215.) The third example is recent: in the summer of 1980 – following an assassination attempt by Jewish terrorists in which Mayor Bassam Shak'a of Nablus lost both his legs and Mayor Karim Khalaf of Ramallah lost a foot – a group of Jewish Nazis gathered in the campus of Tel-Aviv University, roasted a few cats and offered their meat to passers-by as 'shish-kebab from the legs of the Arab mayors'. Anyone who witnessed this macabre orgy – as I did – would have to admit that some horrors defy explanation in the present state of knowledge.

26   One of the early quirks of Jabotinsky (founder of the party then led by Begin) was to propose, in about 1912, the creation of *two* Jewish states, one in Palestine and the other in Angola: the former, being poor in natural resources, would be subsidised by the riches of the latter.

27   Herzl went to Russia to meet von Plehve in August 1903, less than four months after the hideous Kishinev pogrom, for which the latter was known to be responsible. Herzl proposed an alliance, based on their common wish to get most of the Jews out of Russia and, in the shorter term, to divert Jewish support away from the socialist movement. The Tsarist minister started the first interview (8 August) by observing that he regarded himself as 'an ardent supporter of zionism'. When Herzl went on to describe the aims of zionism, von Plehve interrupted: 'You are preaching to the converted'. Amos Elon, *Herzl*, 'Am 'Oved, 1976 pp. 415–9, in Hebrew.

28   Dr Joachim Prinz, *Wir Juden*, Berlin, 1934, pp. 150–1.

29   Ibid., pp. 154–5.

30   For example see ibid., p. 136. Even worse expressions of sympathy with Nazism were voiced by the extremist *Lohamey Herut Yisra'el* (Stern Gang) as late as 1941. Dr Prinz was, in zionist terms, a 'dove'. In the 1970s he even patronised the US Jewish movement *Breira*, until he was dissuaded by Golda Meir.

Chapter 5: The Laws Against Non-Jews

1   Maimonides, *Mishneh Torah*, 'Laws on Murderers' 2, 11; *Talmudic Encyclopedia*, 'Goy'.

2   R. Yo'el Sirkis, *Bayit Hadash*, commentary on *Beyt Josef*, 'Yoreh De'ah' 158. The two rules just mentioned apply even if the Gentile victim is *ger toshav*, that is a 'resident alien' who has undertaken in front of three Jewish witnesses to keep the 'seven Noahide precepts' (seven biblical laws considered by the Talmud to be addressed to Gentiles).

3   R. David Halevi (Poland, 17th century), *Turey Zahav* on *Shulhan 'Arukh*, 'Yoreh De'ah' 158.

4   This concept of 'hostility' will be discussed below.

5   *Talmudic Encyclopedia*, 'Ger' (= convert to Judaism).

6   For example, R. Shabbtay Kohen (mid 17th century), *Siftey Kohen* on *Shulhan 'Arukh*, 'Yoreh De'ah, 158: 'But in times of war it was the custom to kill them with one's own hands, for it is said, "The best of Gentiles – kill him!"' *Siftey Kohen* and *Turey Zahav* (see note 3) are the two major classical commentaries on the *Shulhan 'Arukh*.

7   Colonel Rabbi A. Avidan (Zemel), 'Tohar hannesheq le'or hahalakhah' (= 'Purity of weapons in the light of the Halakhah') in *Be'iqvot milhemet yom hakkippurim – pirqey hagut, halakhah umehqar (In the Wake of the Yom Kippur War – Chapters of Meditation, Halakhah and Research)*, Central Region Command, 1973: quoted in *Ha'olam Hazzeh*, 5 January 1974; also quoted by David Shaham, 'A chapter of meditation', *Hotam*, 28 March 1974; and by Amnon Rubinstein, 'Who falsifies the Halakhah?' *Ma'ariv*, 13 October 1975. Rubinstein reports that the booklet was subsequently withdrawn from circulation by order of the Chief of General Staff, presumably because it encouraged soldiers to disobey his own orders; but he complains that Rabbi Avidan has not been court-martialled, nor has any rabbi – military or civil – taken exception to what he had written.

8   R. Shim'on Weiser, 'Purity of weapons – an exchange of letters' in *Niv Hammidrashiyyah Yearbook* of Midrashiyyat No'am, 1974, pp. 29–31. The yearbook is in Hebrew, English and French, but the material quoted here is printed in Hebrew only.

9   *Psalms*, 42:2.

10   'Thou shalt blot out the remembrance of Amalek from under heaven', *Deuteronomy*, 25:19. Cf. also *I Samuel*, 15:3: 'Now go and smite Amalek, and utterly destroy all that they have, and spare them not; but slay both man and woman, infant and suckling, ox and sheep, camel and ass.'

11   We spare the reader most of these rather convoluted references and quotes from talmudic and rabbinical sources. Such omissions are marked [...]. The rabbi's own conclusions are reproduced in full.

12   The *Tosafot* (literally, Addenda) are a body of scholia to the Talmud, dating from the 11th–13th centuries.

13   Persons guilty of such crimes are even allowed to rise to high public positions. An illustration of this is the case of Shmu'el Lahis, who was responsible for the massacre of between 50 and 75 Arab peasants imprisoned in a mosque after their village had been conquered by the Israeli army during the 1948–9 war. Following a pro forma trial, he was granted complete amnesty, thanks to Ben-Gurion's intercession. The man went on to become a respected lawyer and in the late 1970s was appointed Director General of the Jewish

Agency (which is, in effect, the executive of the zionist movement). In early 1978 the facts concerning his past were widely discussed in the Israeli press, but no rabbi or rabbinical scholar questioned either the amnesty or his fitness for his new office. His appointment was not revoked.

14 *Shulhan 'Arukh*, 'Hoshen Mishpat' 426.

15 Tractate *'Avodah Zarah*, p. 26b.

16 Maimonides, op. cit., 'Murderer' 4, 11.

17 *Leviticus*, 19:16. Concerning the rendering 'thy fellow', see note 14 to Chapter 3.

18 Maimonides, op. cit., 'Idolatry' 10, 1–2.

19 In both cases in section 'Yoreh De'ah' 158. The *Shulhan 'Arukh* repeats the same doctrine in 'Hoshen Mishpat' 425.

20 Moses Rivkes, *Be'er Haggolah* on *Shulhan 'Arukh*, 'Hoshen Mishpat' 425.

21 Thus Professor Jacob Katz, in his Hebrew book *Between Jews and Gentiles* as well as in its more apologetic English version *Exclusiveness and Tolerance*, quotes only this passage verbatim and draws the amazing conclusion that 'regarding the obligation to save life no discrimination should be made between Jew and Christian'. He does not quote any of the authoritative views I have cited above or in the next section.

22 Maimonides, op. cit., 'Sabbath' 2, 20–21; *Shulhan 'Arukh*, 'Orah Hayyim' 329.

23 R 'Aqiva Eiger, commentary on *Shulhan 'Arukh*, ibid. He also adds that if a baby is found abandoned in a town inhabited mainly by Gentiles, a rabbi should be consulted as to whether the baby should be saved.

24 Tractate *'Avodah Zarah*, p. 26.

25 Maimonides, op. cit., 'Sabbath' 2, 12; *Shulhan 'Arukh*, 'Orah Hayyim' 330. The latter text says 'heathen' rather than 'Gentile' but some of the commentators, such as *Turey Zahav*, stress that this ruling applies 'even to Ishmaelites', that is, to Muslims, 'who are not idolators'. Christians are not mentioned explicitly in this connection, but the ruling must *a fortiori* apply to them, since – as we shall see below – Islam is regarded in a more favourable light than Christianity. See also the *responsa* of Hatam Sofer quoted below.

26 These two examples, from Poland and France, are reported by Rabbi I.Z. Cahana (afterwards professor of Talmud in the religious Bar-Ilan University, Israel), 'Medicine in the Halachic post-Talmudic Literature', *Sinai*, vol 27, 1950, p. 221. He also reports the following case from 19th century Italy. Until 1848, a special law in the Papal States banned Jewish doctors from treating Gentiles. The Roman Republic established in 1848 abolished this law along with all other discriminatory law against Jews. But in 1849 an expeditionary

force sent by France's President Louis Napoleon (afterwards Emperor Napoleon III) defeated the Republic and restored Pope Pius IX, who in 1850 revived the anti-Jewish laws. The commanders of the French garrison, disgusted with this extreme reaction, ignored the papal law and hired some Jewish doctors to treat their soldiers. The Chief Rabbi of Rome, Moshe Hazan, who was himself a doctor, was asked whether a pupil of his, also a doctor, could take a job in a French military hospital despite the risk of having to desecrate the sabbath. The rabbi replied that if the conditions of employment expressly mention work on the sabbath, he should refuse. But if they do not, he could take the job and employ 'the great cleverness of God-fearing Jews.' For example, he could repeat on Saturday the prescription given on Friday, by simply telling this to the dispenser. R. Cahana's rather frank article, which contains many other examples, is mentioned in the bibliography of a book by the former Chief Rabbi of Britain, R. Immanuel Jakobovits, *Jewish Medical Ethics*, Bloch, New York, 1962; but in the book itself nothing is said on this matter.

27 *Hokhmat Shlomoh* on *Shulhan 'Arukh*, 'Orah Hayyim' 330, 2.

28 R. Unterman, *Ha'aretz*, 4 April 1966. The only qualification he makes – after having been subjected to continual pressure – is that *in our times* any refusal to give medical assistance to a Gentile could cause such hostility as might endanger Jewish lives.

29 Hatam Sofer, *Responsa* on *Shulhan 'Arukh*, 'Yoreh De'ah' 131.

30 Op. cit., on *Shulhan 'Arukh*, 'Hoshen Mishpat' 194.

31 R. B. Knobelovitz in *The Jewish Review* (Journal of the Mizrachi Party in Great Britain), 8 June 1966.

32 R. Yisra'el Me'ir Kagan – better known as the 'Hafetz Hayyim' – complains in his *Mishnah Berurah*, written in Poland in 1907: 'And know ye that most doctors, even the most religious, do not take any heed whatsoever of this law; for they work on the sabbath and do travel several parasangs to treat a heathen, and they grind medicaments with their own hands. And there is no authority for them to do so. For although we may find it permissible, because of the fear of hostility, to violate bans imposed by the sages – and even this is not clear; yet in bans imposed by the Torah itself it must certainly be forbidden for any Jew to do so, and those who transgress this prohibition violate the sabbath utterly and may God have mercy on them for their sacrilege.' (Commentary on *Shulhan 'Arukh*, 'Orah Hayyim' 330.) The author is generally regarded as the greatest rabbinical authority of his time.

33 Avraham Steinberg MD (ed.), *Jewish Medical Law*, compiled

from *Tzitz Eli'ezer* (*Responsa* of R. Eli'ezer Yehuda Walden-berg), translated by David B. Simons MD, Gefen & Mossad Harav Kook, Jerusalem and California, 1980.

34   Op. cit., p. 39.

35   Ibid., p. 41.

36   Ibid., p. 41. The phrase 'between Jew and gentile' is a euphemism. The dispensation is designed to prevent *hostility of Gentiles towards Jews*, not the other way around.

37   Ibid., p. 41–2; my emphasis.

38   Dr Falk Schlesinger Institute for Medical Halakhic Research at Sha'arey Tzedeq Hospital, *Sefer Asya* (*The Physician's Book*), Reuben Mass, Jerusalem, 1979.

39   By myself in *Ha'olam Hazzeh*, 30 May 1979 and by Shul-lamit Aloni, Member of Knesset, in *Ha'aretz*, 17 June 1980.

40   *Ezekiel*, 23:20.

41   Tractate *Berakhot*, p. 78a.

42   *Talmudic Encyclopedia*, 'Eshet Ish' ('Married Woman').

43   *Exodus*, 20:17.

44   *Genesis*, 2:24.

45   Maimonides, op. cit., 'Prohibitions on Sexual Intercourse' 12, 10; *Talmudic Encyclopedia*, 'Goy'.

46   Maimonides, op. cit., ibid., 12, 1–3. As a matter of fact, every Gentile woman is regarded as *N.Sh.G.Z.* – acronym for the Hebrew words *niddah, shifhah, goyah, zonah* (unpurified from menses, slave, Gentile, prostitute). Upon conversion to Judaism, she ceases indeed to be *niddah, shifhah, goyah* but is still considered *zonah* (prostitute) for the rest of her life, simply by virtue of having been born of a Gentile mother. In a special category is a woman 'conceived not in holiness but born in holiness', that is born to a mother who had con-verted to Judaism while pregnant. In order to make quite sure that there are no mix-ups, the rabbis insist that a married couple who convert to Judaism together must ab-stain from marital relations for three months.

47   Characteristically, an exception to this generalisation is made with respect to Gentiles holding legal office relating to finan-cial transactions: notaries, debt collectors, bailiffs and the like. No similar exception is made regarding ordinary decent Gentiles, not even if they are friendly towards Jews.

48   Some very early (1st century BC) rabbis called this law 'barbaric' and actually returned lost property belonging to Gentiles. But the law nevertheless remained.

49   *Leviticus*, 25:14. This is a literal translation of the Hebrew phrase. The King James Version renders this as 'ye shall not oppress one another'; 'oppress' is imprecise but 'one another' is a correct rendering of the biblical idiom 'each man his

brother'. As pointed out in Chapter 3, the Halakhah interprets all such idioms as referring exclusively to one's fellow Jew.

50 *Shulhan 'Arukh*, 'Hoshen Mishpat' 227.

51 This view is advocated by H. Bar-Droma, *Wezeh Gvul Ha'aretz* (*And This Is the Border of the Land*), Jerusalem, 1958. In recent years this book is much used by the Israeli army in indoctrinating its officers.

52 Maimonides, op. cit., 'Idolatry' 10, 3–4.

53 See note 2.

54 *Exodus*, 23:33.

55 Maimonides, op. cit., 'Idolatry' 10, 6.

56 *Deuteronomy*, 20:16. See also the verses quoted in note 10.

57 *Numbers* 31:13–20; note in particular verse 17: 'Now therefore kill every male among the little ones, and kill every woman that hath known man by lying with him.'

58 R. Sha'ul Yisra'eli, 'Taqrit Qibbiya Le'or Hahalakhah' (The Qibbiya incident in the light of the Halakhah'), in *Hattorah Wehammedinah*, vol 5, 1953/4.

59 This is followed by a blessing 'for not making me a slave'. Next, a male must add a blessing 'for not making me a woman', and a female 'for making me as He pleased'.

60 In eastern Europe it was until recent times a universal custom among Jews to spit on the floor at this point, as an expression of scorn. This was not however a strict obligation, and today the custom is kept only by the most pious.

61 The Hebrew word is *meshummadim*, which in rabbinical usage refers to Jews who become 'idolators', that is either pagan or Christians, but not to Jewish converts to Islam.

62 The Hebrew word is *minim*, whose precise meaning is 'disbelievers in the uniqueness of God'.

63 Tractate *Berakhot*, p. 58b.

64 According to many rabbinical authorities the original rule still applies in full in the Land of Israel.

65 This custom gave rise to many incidents in the history of European Jewry. One of the most famous, whose consequence is still visible today, occurred in 14th century Prague. King Charles IV of Bohemia (who was also Holy Roman Emperor) had a magnificent crucifix erected in the middle of a stone bridge which he had built and which still exists today. It was then reported to him that the Jews of Prague are in the habit of spitting whenever they pass next to the crucifix. Being a famous protector of the Jews, he did not institute persecution against them, but simply sentenced the Jewish community to pay for the Hebrew word *Adonay* (Lord) to be inscribed on the crucifix in golden letters. This

word is one of the seven holiest names of God, and no mark of disrespect is allowed in front of it. The spitting ceased. Other incidents connected with the same custom were much less amusing.

66   The verses most commonly used for this purpose contain words derived from the Hebrew root *shaqetz* which means 'abominate, detest', as in *Deuteronomy*, 7:26: 'thou shalt utterly detest it, and thou shalt utterly abhor it; for it is a cursed thing.' It seems that the insulting term *sheqetz*, used to refer to all Gentiles (Chapter 2), originated from this custom.

67   *Talmud*, Tractate *Beytzah*, p. 21a, b; *Mishnah Berurah* on *Shulhan 'Arukh*, 'Orah Hayyim' 512. Another commentary (*Magen Avraham*) also excludes Karaites.

68   According to the Halakhah, a Gentile slave bought by a Jew should be converted to Judaism, but does not thereby become a proper Jew.

69   *Leviticus*, 25:46.

70   The Hebrew form of the name Jesus – *Yeshu* – was interpreted as an acronym for the curse 'may his name and memory be wiped out', which is used as an extreme form of abuse. In fact, anti-zionist Orthodox Jews (such as Neturey Qarta) sometimes refer to Herzl as 'Herzl Jesus' and I have found in religious zionist writings expressions such as 'Nasser Jesus' and more recently 'Arafat Jesus'.

INDEX